Study MAX

For my son, Joshua Ryan Greene
Your spirit and zest still enthrall me.
I shall always be thankful for the joy you have brought into my life.

Lawrence J. Greene

Study MAX

Improving Study Skills in Grades 9-12

CORWIN PRESS
A Sage Publications Company
Thousand Oaks, California

Selected material from Unit 1 has been paraphrased and modified from *Study Wise: A Program for Maximizing Your Learning Potential* by Lawrence J. Greene. Copyright © 2004. Adapted by permission of Pearson Education, Inc., Upper Saddle River, NJ.

Student portions of this book are designed for classroom use and may be reproduced by the individual educators and local school sites who have purchased the book.

For information:

Corwin Press
A Sage Publications Company
2455 Teller Road
Thousand Oaks, California 91320
www.corwinpress.com

Sage Publications Ltd.
1 Oliver's Yard
55 City Road
London, EC1Y 1SP
United Kingdom

Sage Publication India Pvt. Ltd.
B-42, Panchsheel Enclave
Post Box 4109
New Delhi 110 017 India

Printed in the United States of America

Library of Congress Cataloging-in-Publication Data

Greene, Lawrence J.
Study Max : improving study skills in grades 9-12 / by Lawrence J. Greene.
        p. cm.
Includes bibliographical references and index.
ISBN 1-4129-0467-6 (cloth) — ISBN 1-4129-0468-4 (pbk.)
    1. Study skills—Handbooks, manuals, etc. 2. High school teaching—Handbooks, manuals, etc. I. Title.

LB1601.G737 2005
373.13'028'1—dc22

                                        2004015932

This book is printed on acid-free paper.

05   06   07   08   09   10   9   8   7   6   5   4   3   2   1

Acquisitions Editor:	Faye Zucker
Editorial Assistants:	Stacy Wagner, Gem Rabanera
Production Editor:	Julia Parnell
Copy Editor:	Elizabeth Budd
Typesetter:	C&M Digitals (P) Ltd.
Proofreader:	Sally Scott
Indexer:	Kay M. Dusheck
Cover Designer:	Tracy E. Miller
Production Artist:	Katherine Minerva

Contents

Acknowledgments

Joshua Ryan Greene, my nine-year-old son, deserves a heartfelt acknowledgment for letting me use "his" computer. Those many mornings when he entertained himself with construction projects and allowed me to write were a blessing and are much appreciated. Dan and Evelyn Greene, as always, were there for me with their unconditional love and support. And so, too, were Evan and Lisa Greene. Thank you all.

Corwin Press extends its thanks to David Scheidecker for the analysis and encouragement he provided as a manuscript reviewer.

About the Author

Lawrence J. Greene, a graduate of the Stanford University Graduate School of Education, is a nationally recognized author, educational therapist, and curriculum developer who has worked with more than 10,000 struggling students during a clinical career spanning thirty years. He has written 18 books, and he has trained thousands of teachers in graduate programs at the university level. His educational curricula are currently used in elementary schools, middle schools, high schools, colleges, and universities throughout the world, and his books have been translated into languages ranging from Chinese to Spanish.

Other books by Lawrence J. Greene include:

Kids Who Hate School
Kids Who Underachieve
Learning Disabilities and Your Child
Getting Smarter
Think Smart, Study Smart
Smarter Kids
Teachers' Desk Reference Guide to Learning Problems
1001 Ways to Improve Your Child's Schoolwork
Improving Your Child's Schoolwork
The Life-Smart Kid
Finding Help When Your Child Is Struggling in School
Roadblocks to Learning
Winning the Study Game
Study Wise
The Resistant Learner
Helping Kids Fix Problems and Avoid Crises (forthcoming from Corwin Press)

Introduction

For Teachers

The widely held belief that intelligence is the primary determinant in school success discounts the key roles that motivation, focused effort, and effective study skills play in the academic achievement equation. Although it's true that the ability to grasp concepts, understand abstractions, perceive relationships, and recall information can facilitate learning and enhance school performance, it's also true that a superior IQ does not guarantee superior academic achievement. Intellectually gifted students may perform marginally in school while their less gifted classmates may do exceptionally well.

That *natural or inherited intelligence* (IQ) isn't the exclusive determinant in academic success is apparent to anyone with teaching experience. Another key factor must be added to the scholastic achievement equation. This factor, which is best described as *applied intelligence* (AI),* involves the practical, strategic, and tactical utilization of available resources. Students who have good academic and study skills, who target personally meaningful goals, who develop a functional plan for proceeding from Point A to Point B to Point C, and who work diligently to achieve their objectives invariably excel in school. These students are clearly identifiable, and the benchmark that distinguishes them is that they're in school to learn. They have a sense of purpose and direction. They possess the requisite learning tools, and they deliberately and consistently use these tools.

Successful students share a range of key characteristics that distinguish them from marginally performing and nonperforming classmates. These students

- Identify and capitalize on their learning preferences, strengths, and natural aptitudes.
- Manage time efficiently.
- Plan ahead.
- Organize their study environment.

Applied intelligence (AI) is a term coined by the author. As yet, no quantitative, standardized instrument exists for measuring AI.

- Record homework assignments accurately.
- Complete their work.
- Meet deadlines.
- Proofread their work carefully.
- Read with good comprehension.
- Identify important information when studying.
- Develop an effective system for recalling key data.
- Take effective notes from textbooks and lectures.
- Study and learn actively.
- Anticipate what's likely to be asked on tests.

In addition to these functional scholastic capabilities, achieving students also share other key success-enhancing characteristics. They

- Establish personally meaningful goals.
- Set priorities.
- Develop strategies and tactics for attaining their objectives.
- Consider the potential consequences of their attitudes and behavior.
- Avoid or neutralize problems.
- Handle setbacks.
- Learn from mistakes.
- Weigh their options.
- Manifest good judgment.

Can students be taught these success-oriented study skills and life skills, and can the instruction be integrated into the curriculum without teachers having to make major content area sacrifices? You bet they can! Virtually all students can be trained to learn more efficiently and study more productively. The payoffs for students possessing these capacities are immense and include improved academic self-confidence, enhanced pride, superior motivation, expanded educational and career opportunities, and elevated expectations and aspirations.*

As a frontline educator, no one need tell you that students who study effectively have a major advantage over those who spin their wheels with little traction and forward momentum. Successful students, in effect, join an elite club whose members are on a track leading to higher education and rewarding careers, and their achievements significantly increase the likelihood that they'll ultimately take their place at the top of the economic and vocational food chain.

Unfortunately, many potentially capable students never make it into the elite club because no one has taught them how to learn and study productively. These marginally performing, and in many cases demoralized, defeated, and resistant, teenagers are destined to muddle through high school in a cerebral haze. They're also destined to arrive at the end of the educational production line with dulled intellect, substandard skills, tenuous self-confidence, and limited educational and career prospects.

---

*Please note: Life skills are addressed in the *Life Skills Workbook* (Greene, Corwin Press, in press).

Is the Ability to Achieve Inherited?

Some students discover on their own how to learn effectively without requiring formal study skills instruction. Whether these "natural" students acquire their insights intuitively, through careful observation, or by consciously or unconsciously modeling their behavior and attitudes on those of their achieving parents, siblings, role models, or peers is open to debate.

Natural students represent a relatively small percentage of the high school population. Those who don't figure out how to learn productively are often tagged as lacking in ability or as underachievers, and those who become resistant to learning are usually identified as having "an attitude." Left to their own devices, these students typically tread water for four years and do little more than go through the motions of learning. Some turn off and shut down. Some do little more than take up space in the classroom. Others act out and become behavior problems. Before these students can realistically be expected to work conscientiously and function at a level commensurate with their actual ability, they must be furnished with the tools they need to succeed academically.

You may be thinking, "Hold on! Given content area curriculum requirements, is it realistic to expect already overburdened teachers to carve out time for instructing students in how to study more productively?" The answer to this question is *yes.* The teaching can be done quickly and efficiently and with minimal disruption. Teachers can pick and choose the specific components they want to teach, and they can devote as few as four hours to as many as twenty hours during the semester to providing the instruction. The payoffs in terms of enhanced learning and performance will more than justify this investment in time and effort.

Passive Learning

Many nonperforming and underperforming students share a notable trait: *They learn passively.* Studying translates into little more than a mindless procedure of turning the pages in their textbooks while occasionally glancing at their class notes, assuming, of course, they've actually bothered to take decipherable notes. The consequences of this passive learning are predictable and include deficient skills, minimal mastery of course content, and poor grades.

Students who muddle through four years of high school often bear emotional scars that attest to their less-than-stellar academic experiences. Frustration, test anxiety, learning phobias, and deficient self-confidence are the common by-products of this struggle. Having no evidence to the contrary, these ineffectual learners are likely to devalue their intelligence, discount their abilities, and reduce their ambitions. They're also like to conclude, consciously or unconsciously, that they're inadequate.

Marginally performing students often choose the path of least resistance and do everything possible to avoid studying. Deluding themselves that they aren't really doing poorly if they aren't really trying, they simply deny that they have any problems. The litany of excuses, responsibility-deflecting complaints, and rationalizations frequently includes the following:

1. School is dumb.

2. The information is useless.

3. The teacher is a jerk.

4. The tests are unfair.

Wizened teachers are not fooled by these transparent justifications for minimal effort and marginal performance that ironically call attention to the very insufficiencies that these students are attempting to hide.

It's axiomatic that students with the greatest need to study are usually the most resistant to studying. They're often disorganized and unmotivated. They procrastinate and submit sloppy, incomplete assignments. They miss deadlines and blame others for their difficulties. Their maladaptive attitudes and behavior magnify their deficiencies, but they're too enmeshed in their defensive system to perceive this. One doesn't require a crystal ball to see that these students are destined to crash against monumental barriers not only in school, but also in the harsh and demanding world beyond school.

A compelling argument can be made for providing all students with systematic study skills instruction as an integral component in their education. Logic suggests that this instruction be furnished in elementary school before self-defeating habits, counterproductive attitudes, and self-sabotaging behaviors become entrenched. Unfortunately, logic doesn't always prevail in our educational system, and every year vast numbers of teenagers enter high school with abysmal study habits.

Perhaps as many as 40 percent of high school students are functioning below their full academic potential. Some spin their wheels without generating forward momentum. Some don't study. Some don't complete their homework or submit their assignments on time. Others express their frustration and demoralization by acting out in class and being disruptive. Others suppress their frustration and demoralization and retreat into their daydreams. That these students often identify with and gravitate toward peers who are also doing poorly in school should not surprise us. The subculture functions as an oasis from pressure to perform and expectations that cannot be met and reinforces shared negative attitudes, maladaptive behavior, and nihilistic values.

The Achievement Loop

Academic achievement is, in effect, a recycling loop. Good skills in tandem with goals, motivation, effort, desire, and self-confidence produce successful students. This success, in turn, encourages students to establish new goals and generates motivation, effort, desire, and self-confidence. The more students accomplish, the more they believe in themselves, and the more they believe in themselves, the more they'll want to continue achieving. The resulting pride and sense of personal efficacy are addictive. Students will want to continue achieving because they enjoy the feelings associated with achievement and desire more of the same. Once they're acclimated to success, they'll conclude that they *can* succeed and that they *deserve* to succeed.

The interactive dynamics of the achievement loop can be graphically represented as follows:

The Achievement Loop

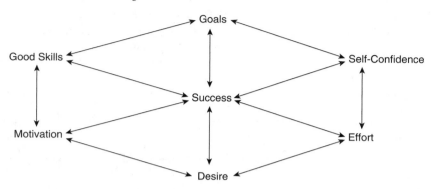

Just as achievement is a recycling loop, so, too, is nonachievement. Poor skills, the absence of goals, deficient desire, inadequate motivation, diminished self-confidence, and little effort produce little or no success. Little or no success, in turn, generates diminished self-confidence, deficient desire, and inadequate motivation, which, in turn, guarantee continued marginal performance. In other words, the more students do poor poorly in school, the less faith they have in themselves and the less willing they are to assert themselves and stretch for the academic brass ring. To extricate themselves from this nonachievement loop, marginally performing and nonperforming students must be provided with the tools they need to get the job done.

The interactive dynamics of the nonachievement loop can also be represented graphically:

The Nonachievement Loop

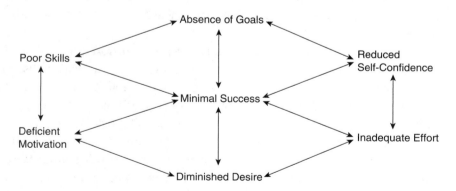

Note that the arrows connecting the components in both loops point in two directions and that an arrow from each component also points to the center of the loop. This representation underscores how each element in the dynamic has an impact on the other elements.

Students who have faith in their ability to solve problems, meet challenges, and achieve academically are motivated, goal directed, and emotionally resilient. They radiate self-assurance, bounce back from defeats and disappointments, prevail over challenges, and attain their goals.

Students who are academically defeated are at the opposite end of the potency continuum. They are dispirited, unmotivated, frustrated, uninvolved in learning, emotionally fragile, and psychologically defended.

Description of Content

The **Study Max** Program provides a step-by-step methodology for helping students become fully engaged learners. The program is based on the premise that students can be taught virtually fail-safe procedures for achieving academically.

The reproducible components consist of an introduction and three instructional sections. In the **Introduction,** students complete a comprehensive study skills profile, interpret their responses, evaluate their performance in each subject, and list their personal improvement goals. This procedure permits students to acquire insight into their academic modus operandi and provides baseline data that can be compared with subsequent data after students complete the program.

Part 1: Learning Styles and Preferences consists of a single unit that's designed to help students identify their learning strengths and their intelligence type. **Part 2: Getting Organized** consists of Units 2–5 and focuses on helping students create an organized, time-efficient study system and a conducive environment for effective learning. **Part 3: Turbo Charging Reading and Studying,** consists of Units 6–10 and focuses on helping students acquire the specific academic skills that are requisite to productive studying and effective test preparation. Students learn how to speed read, improve their reading comprehension, take effective textbook and class notes, identify important information, understand concepts, recall facts, anticipate what is likely to be on tests, and write powerful, well-organized essays that clearly express and encapsulate key information.

The Study Max Program contains more than one hundred highly focused exercises and activities that concentrate on providing practical skills with immediate applications. These exercises and activities encourage students to become introspective and more aware of their own proclivities when studying. Repeated opportunities for practice, reinforcement, and mastery are integrated into the instructional methodology. Students are "set up to succeed," and these intentionally engineered successes are designed to generate self-confidence and stimulate effort and motivation. The objective is to empower students by teaching them easy- to-learn and easy-to-apply skills, stimulating their strategic thinking and energizing their intellectual development.

As previously stated, you can choose the specific components of the program that you want to integrate into your curriculum. Another option is to offer a dedicated study skills program as an elective, a summer school program, or an after-school tutorial program. Although most students should be able to complete many of the activities independently or with minimal guidance, the program is designed to be teacher-student interactive, and the content is intended to be examined and discussed in class.

The Instructional Method

The **Study Max Program** incorporates an instructional method called **cognitive behavioral change.** This teaching technique is based on six teaching principles:

1. *Relevancy*—the skills directly relate to the challenges that students confront every day.

2. *Insight*—the program demonstrates that the skills being taught can make school easier, more productive, and more rewarding.

3. *Instruction*—the methods are presented systematically and sequenced to ensure comprehension.

4. *Reinforcement*—the program offers repeated opportunities to practice to ensure mastery and assimilation.

5. *Behavior Modification*—the methods develop productive behaviors through methodical practice and carefully orchestrated opportunities for success.

6. *Application*—the program offers repeated opportunities to use the skills being taught to ensure habituation.

The goal of this systematic instructional process is to guide students to the realization that the skills they're learning are valuable and that mastery of these skills can make their lives easier and more productive and rewarding. This critically important paradigm shift from passive learning to active learning is essential to improved academic performance.

How to Use This Resource

In the teacher section that precedes each unit, the underlying pedagogical issues that relate to the topics being presented are succinctly examined. You'll find an overview of the objectives for the unit, a lesson plan, and a description of each activity.

In the student sections, case studies are designed to help students acquire insight through a methodical examination and analysis of the modus operandi of students with whom they can most likely identify. This use of anecdotal surrogates is intended to make the self-examination process less threatening to teenagers who are defensive and resistant to introspection. The reproducible exercises provide repeated opportunities for students to practice each skill being taught until the skill has been fully mastered and assimilated. The goal is for students to integrate the insights and skills and to develop a highly functional and personalized study system.

You may choose to read certain sections aloud to the class, or you may prefer that students take turns reading aloud. Some exercises are optional and can either be done in class or assigned as homework. These optional exercises can be used to reinforce concepts and skills or can be used for remedial purposes with students who are struggling.

This program deliberately encourages students to "stretch" intellectually. This stretching process is intended to stimulate academic and intellectual growth, but it can also produce frustration and discouragement if at-risk students are initially asked to reach too far. Struggling students who have decoding, focusing, reading comprehension, or vocabulary difficulties may require more individualized help and monitoring to master certain of the targeted skills and concepts. By avoiding excessive demands, reducing the number of assigned activities, and extending completion deadlines, you can significantly reduce the likelihood of undermining their self-esteem and triggering defensiveness and resistance.*

Recommended Instructional Guidelines

1. Examine the content of each chapter carefully before presenting the material.

2. Resist being highly critical or judgmental.

3. Show respect for students' viewpoints even if they appear off target. (If these viewpoints indicate maladaptive thinking, you'll want to reorient this thinking incrementally while being aware of and sensitive to differing cultural values.)

4. Encourage students to think analytically, critically, and strategically and require that they be able to defend their position logically. (This will develop and enhance reasoning skills, insight, and communication skills.)

5. Provide support, encouragement, and affirmation for progress and communicate positive expectations!

The **Study Skills Profile** in the Introduction is designed to help students assess their current study skills, attitudes, performance, and goals. Classes comprising highly motivated and academically advanced students might benefit from discussing their completed profile at the onset. This discussion could lead to their targeting more precisely what they want from the program.

If students respond to the self-assessments forthrightly, a considerable number of those in mainstream classes (as distinct from advanced placement classes) will probably indicate deficient study habits. These students may be self-conscious and embarrassed and may not want to discuss their profiles in front of their classmates. Those who are psychologically defended may even try to make a joke out of the self-assessment exercise, and any attempt to examine their attitudes and behavior at the onset could cause them to become even more defensive

---

*See *Winning the Study Game* (Greene, 2003). This study skills program is specifically designed for students participating in middle school and high school resource programs.

and resistant. For these reasons, you may elect not to initiate immediately an in-depth class discussion of the self-assessments. If you do decide to proceed with a class discussion, student participation should be voluntary.

If you have a core of reluctant or resistant learners in your class, it's recommended that you put off discussing the profiles until after the class has completed the components you've selected. At the end of the program, students could complete the profile again and compare their initial responses with their subsequent responses. The comparisons are likely to trigger a lively class discussion. Once students have assimilated more productive behavior, attitudes, and skills, they should be more willing to examine and compare their pre- and postprofile responses.

It's time to get started.

Introduction

For Students

*T*his *program is designed to make your life easier.* It will teach you how to study, think, and plan more effectively. If you use the techniques, you'll be able to learn more efficiently, and your grades will improve.

There is a payoff for doing well in school: **You'll have more choices when you graduate from high school.** Some of you may be planning to go to a university or community college. Others may be planning to learn a trade. Others among you may be undecided about your future educational and career plans.

Thinking about what you want to do with your life while you're still in high school may seem a bit weird. But before you know it, you'll have graduated high school, and you'll be faced with important decisions about how you're going to earn a living and how you're going to find satisfaction and fulfillment in your work. Whatever your career goals are, *knowing how to learn is a powerful tool that you'll be able to use throughout your life.* To advance in whatever field you choose, you must be able to understand, recall, and apply new information. Ask any pilot, accountant, attorney, technician, actor, mechanic, software developer, professional soldier, hotel administrator, dancer, physician, police officer, or scientist, and they'll confirm a basic fact of life in the real world: *You're on a dead-end street if you do not continually acquire new capabilities.* The list includes technical skills, computer skills, problem-solving skills, and learning skills.

Before beginning the *Study Max Program,* take a few minutes to complete the following **Study Skills Profile.** It will help you understand how you're currently studying. This is not a test, and you will not be graded on your answers. The information is for your own use. So answer as honestly as you can. At the end of the profile, you'll find information that will allow you to interpret your responses to the statements and questions in the profile.

Study Skills Profile

Part 1: Study Skills Inventory

	USUALLY	SOMETIMES	RARELY
I'm motivated to do well in school and get good grades.	_____	_____	_____
I'm motivated in school.	_____	_____	_____
I'm well organized.	_____	_____	_____
I bring home the materials I need to do my homework.	_____	_____	_____
I record my assignments every day on an assignment sheet.	_____	_____	_____
I avoid listening to loud music or watching TV when I study.	_____	_____	_____
I spend adequate time studying and doing homework.	_____	_____	_____
I study without a lot of interruptions.	_____	_____	_____
I do my work without procrastinating.	_____	_____	_____
I can concentrate when studying.	_____	_____	_____
I understand and can follow written directions.	_____	_____	_____
I understand and can follow verbal directions.	_____	_____	_____
I can work independently.	_____	_____	_____
I have a written study schedule that I follow.	_____	_____	_____
I plan ahead.	_____	_____	_____
I manage my time well.	_____	_____	_____
I consistently complete my assignments.	_____	_____	_____
I consistently submit my assignments on time.	_____	_____	_____
I allow time to check over my work to find errors.	_____	_____	_____

I establish short-term goals
(example: a B+ on the next history test).   _____   _____   _____

I establish long-term goals
(example: an A in history).   _____   _____   _____

I establish priorities (list my obligations
in order of importance).   _____   _____   _____

I think about what career or
vocation I would like to pursue.   _____   _____   _____

I can understand the
content in my textbooks.   _____   _____   _____

I can remember what I read.   _____   _____   _____

I know how to identify important
information when studying.   _____   _____   _____

I can recall key information
when I take a test.   _____   _____   _____

I feel confident when taking tests.   _____   _____   _____

I take good class notes.   _____   _____   _____

I take good textbook notes.   _____   _____   _____

I can figure out what my teachers
are likely to ask on tests.   _____   _____   _____

I can study intensively for twenty-five
minutes without a break.   _____   _____   _____

I know how to review and study
effectively for tests.   _____   _____   _____

I have confidence in my academic skills.   _____   _____   _____

I make my best effort in school.   _____   _____   _____

I'm truthful when telling my parents
I've done my homework.   _____   _____   _____

I'm satisfied with my grades.   _____   _____   _____

I'm satisfied with my current study skills.   _____   _____   _____

Part 2: Using Scales to Evaluate Your Performance

Rate your overall current performance in school:

1	2	3	4	5	6	7	8	9	10
Poor			Average				Excellent		

Rate how pleased you are with your grades:

1	2	3	4	5	6	7	8	9	10
Not Pleased			**Somewhat Pleased**				**Very Pleased**		

Rate your overall effort in school:

1	2	3	4	5	6	7	8	9	10
Poor			**Average**				**Excellent**		

How much total time do you spend doing homework on a typical school night? _____

Rate your current performance in each of your subjects. (If the school year has just started and you haven't yet received any grades, rate yourself in the subjects you took last year.)

Subject:

Quality of your overall work in this subject:

1	2	3	4	5	6	7	8	9	10
Poor			**Average**				**Excellent**		

Subject: _____

Quality of your overall work in this subject:

1	2	3	4	5	6	7	8	9	10
Poor			**Average**				**Excellent**		

Subject: _____

Quality of your overall work in this subject:

1	2	3	4	5	6	7	8	9	10
Poor			**Average**				**Excellent**		

Subject: _____

Quality of your overall work in this subject:

1	2	3	4	5	6	7	8	9	10
Poor			**Average**				**Excellent**		

Subject: _____

Quality of your overall work in this subject:

1	2	3	4	5	6	7	8	9	10
Poor			**Average**				**Excellent**		

Rate your current attitude about school.

1	2	3	4	5	6	7	8	9	10
Poor			**Average**				**Excellent**		

Rate your overall abilities.

1	2	3	4	5	6	7	8	9	10
Poor			**Average**				**Excellent**		

Part 3: Personal Improvement Goals

Check the areas in which you would like to improve your skills:

_____ Identifying important information when studying

_____ Memorizing important facts

_____ Understanding information in textbooks

_____ Understanding information presented in class (lectures, discussions, etc.)

_____ Completing homework within a reasonable amount of time

_____ Improving essay-writing skills

_____ Studying for tests

_____ Organizing schoolwork

_____ Organizing your at-home study environment

_____ Budgeting and scheduling time

_____ Planning ahead

_____ Improving concentration

_____ Taking notes in class

_____ Taking notes from textbooks

_____ Participating effectively in class discussions

_____ Handling test anxiety

_____ Figuring out what is likely to be asked on tests

_____ Developing problem-solving skills

_____ Improving performance on multiple-choice and short-answer tests

_____ Improving performance on essay tests

_____ Becoming motivated

_____ Improving academic self-confidence

_____ Improving grades

List the specific target grades you would like to receive on your next report card (be realistic!):

Subject: _____ **Grade:** _____

Subject: _____ **Grade:** _____

Subject: _____ **Grade:** _____

Subject: _____ **Grade:** _____

Subject: _____ **Grade:** _____

Interpreting Your Responses to the Profile

Study Skill Inventory

If you checked "rarely" in response to more than two of the statements on the inventory or you checked "sometimes" to more than five statements, the Study Max Program can play a major role in improving your school performance. Even if you checked "usually" to most of the statements, you'll undoubtedly benefit from this study skills enhancement program. The objective is to hone your skills. This will provide a competitive edge that will serve you in high school and in college.

Performance Evaluation Scales

If your evaluation of your current skills, attitudes, and performance indicates problem areas (that is, you circled "1," "2," or "3" in assessing your work in specific subjects), the Study Max Program can play a major role in improving your performance in these areas. The program can also enhance your attitude and overall performance.

If your evaluation of your current skills, attitudes, and performance indicates below average to slightly above average skills, attitudes, and performance (that is, you circled "4," "5," "6," or "7"), the Study Max Program can help your fine-tune your study skills and bump them into the superior range.

If your skills are already in the superior range (that is, "8," "9," or "10"), there is still room for improvement. With enhanced skills, B+ and A– students can become straight-A students, and A students can become A+ students. It's simply a question of having the necessary tools and motivation.

If you are displeased with the results of your profile, don't be discouraged. Temporarily suspend judgment about your abilities. You'll have opportunities to correct the deficiencies. Your teacher may choose to discuss your responses now or to put off discussing the inventory and self-evaluation scales until later.

Let's get started. You're about to learn how to power charge your studying and add additional horsepower and torque to your mental engine.

Part 1

Learning Styles
and Preferences

Unit 1

Figuring Out How Students Learn Best

For Teachers

Objectives

This unit helps students identify their learning strengths, learning preferences, and distinctive intelligence type and encourages them to capitalize on their natural capabilities when they learn and study.

LESSON PLAN

1. Students read the introductory case study titled **Getting the Most Out of What You've Got.** They identify and evaluate each of the protagonist's school-related behaviors and attitudes and predict the consequences.

2. In **Identifying Your Own Learning Preferences,** students complete a **Personal Learning Modality Inventory** and interpret their responses.
   - In **Using Different Learning Modalities,** students examine the unique characteristics of five major learning styles, explore ideas for maximizing studying and learning effectiveness, and consider how they might use each modality when studying.
   - In **Figuring Out Your Intelligence Type,** students examine nine types of intelligence and amplify on how each might be used.

- In **Taking Stock**, students apply what they've discovered about their learning strengths, preferred learning modality or modalities, and intelligence type and describe how they might use this information to improve their school performance and orient themselves vocationally.

LEARNING PREFERENCES

Successful students intuitively identify and capitalize on their dominant learning modality or modalities when they study. They may not necessarily be consciously aware of how they learn best and why they study in a particular way, but they instinctively exploit their innate strengths and talents whenever possible.

In contrast, underperforming students rarely establish this cause-and-effect link between scholastic achievement and the strategic utilization of their natural abilities. Most of these students don't realize that they can intentionally apply their innate learning strengths and preferences to assimilate information, master skills, and compensate for any academic deficiencies they might have. For example, an auditory learner who has difficulty assimilating visual data in textbooks or lecture notes might detour around this limitation by recording important information on an audio cassette, capitalizing on his auditory learning strength, and repeatedly listening to the content. Another option would be for the student to deliver "pretend" lectures that encapsulate the key content to an imaginary class. By verbalizing and by hearing himself lecturing, he could use his strength—the auditory modality—to imprint the information he needs to learn. The student might also orally ask himself test questions when studying and could answer the questions aloud, or, in preparing for a test, he and a study partner could ask each other challenging oral questions and answer them.

Marginally performing students who are unaware that there are viable learning modality alternatives for assimilating information are likely to persist in using their ineffectual study procedures despite unequivocal evidence that these methods are failing. The consequences are predictable: continued marginal performance and demoralization.

Students who learn how to identify and then intentionally capitalize on their abilities and preferences can exert positive control over what happens to them in the scholastic arena. Their insights about how they assimilate information most effectively will provide them with a personal and distinctive "learning identity." They can proclaim, "I'm an experiential learner, and I can use this talent to get better grades." This new mind set can revitalize a deflated self-concept that's been repeatedly bruised by negative school experiences.

MULTIPLE INTELLIGENCES

Recognizing significant limitations in traditional IQ assessments, Harvard professor Howard Gardner has developed a more comprehensive model for defining intelligence. Contending that many different types of intelligence are not measured or acknowledged by an IQ test, he has coined the term *Multiple*

Intelligences and has identified nine major areas of natural ability. (These are described in the student section of this unit.)

The nine types of intelligence identified by Gardner significantly broaden the conventional intelligence-testing paradigm. The extended model acknowledges and affirms capabilities that are not factored into the traditional assessment of intelligence. According to Gardner's new paradigm, Michael Jordan, Michelle Kwan, Tom Hanks, Bill Gates, or Ray Romano should be considered as brilliant in their fields as acknowledged intellectual luminaries such as Madame Curie, Louis Pasteur, or Albert Einstein were in theirs. Despite Gardner's amplification of how intelligence is conceptualized, traditional IQ tests are still widely used, and as yet no standardized protocol exists for qualitatively and quantitatively assessing multiple intelligences.

Gardner's insights have particular relevance in the case of underperforming students. By helping students discover their distinctive talents (previously described as aptitudes) and by validating, acknowledging, and affirming their capabilities, teachers can play a pivotal role in enhancing the self-concept of these students. Armed with new insights, teenagers who previously perceived themselves as academically inadequate can begin to reappraise their self-worth. Even resistant and learning-aversive students are likely to discover that they are far more capable than they ever believed.

Multiple intelligences and preferred or dominant learning modalities are clearly interrelated and overlapping. Students who possess superior verbal/linguistic intelligence would most likely prefer to use the auditory modality when learning, and students who possess superior visual/spatial intelligence would most likely prefer to use the visual modality. A tactile or kinesthetic learner is likely to have superior bodily/kinesthetic intelligence and whenever feasible would probably prefer to capitalize on this type of intelligence. In each instance, the student's dominant learning modality would in all likelihood correspond to the student's distinctive intelligence type.

Key Questions About Your Students' Abilities and Performance

- Do I have a responsibility to help students identify their natural talents, aptitudes, and learning strengths and preferences?
- Could some of my students actually be more capable than I've previously believed?
- Could my students perform at a higher level if they were able to identify and capitalize on their natural capabilities?
- If students acquire greater insight about their natural talents and are taught how to capitalize on these talents, could this enhance their self-esteem, academic self-confidence, motivation, and effort?

If you've answered these questions affirmatively, then you'll recognize the value of examining this unit with your students. The content may also provide an additional payoff. You may actually gain new insight into your *own* personal learning style, preferences, teaching style, and intelligence type. Teachers generally emphasize their own strengths and preferences when they teach, although they may not be consciously aware that they're doing so. For example, teachers who are visual learners and who possess natural visual intelligence are likely to emphasize the recall of information found in textbooks and encapsulated in class notes. Teachers who are experiential learners would tend to emphasize hands-on learning and experimentation. A thought to consider: Would you be willing to integrate instructional components that correspond to a broad range of student learning styles so that students who learn differently from you might also have an engineered opportunity to excel in your class?

USING MULTIPLE MODALITIES

Although students' identification of their learning strengths, preferences, and distinctive intelligence type can have a positive impact on their learning efficacy and academic self-confidence, students must also recognize that in certain learning situations, it may be more strategic for them to use a nondominant modality. For example, an auditory learner may prefer to learn French verb conjugations by reciting them aloud and incorporating the conjugations in spoken dialogues (an auditory process). She may conclude, however, that it would be more effective for her to learn chemistry symbols by writing them on flash cards and by repeatedly reciting then aloud while also reading them silently (a procedure that combines both auditory and visual learning). The ability to select the right learning tool for a particular job is an example of pragmatic tactical thinking. Successful students will use whatever methodology works best in a particular learning situation. To get the job done, sometimes they may need a screwdriver, and sometimes they may need a wrench.

Although students should capitalize on their natural learning strengths and aptitudes, they should also be able to use nonpreferred modalities. For example, auditory, tactile, kinesthetic, and experiential learners can be taught how to use the visual modality when expedient. These students can be taught how to imprint visual pictures when they study by looking intently at a block of information, closing their eyes, and trying to visualize the data (these techniques are examined on page 188). With sufficient effort and practice, students can train themselves to *see* a chemical formula or an irregular Spanish conjugation imprinted on the inside of their eyelids. By so doing, they're developing, enhancing, and utilizing their visual memory skills.

With equivalent intention, visual learners can enhance their auditory capabilities. For example, they might imagine that they're "burning" an audio CD in their mind as they recite Spanish dialogues aloud. By making a concerted effort to vocalize and hear themselves rhythmically recite the dialogues, they are deliberately developing, enhancing, and utilizing the auditory modality to assimilate the assigned material. So, too, might visual and auditory learners enhance their tactile and experiential learning skills and learning effectiveness by deliberately utilizing hands-on learning experiences. For example, they might use a skeleton in their biology classroom to help them identify and remember major bones in the body. In chemistry class, they might manipulate the configuration an atomic model and in this way better understand and assimilate the physical principles that they are required to master.

You want your students to capitalize on their natural learning talents, but you also want them to recognize when they should strategically use other methods. This ability to utilize multiple learning resources is a primary benchmark of the academically successful student.

SUMMARY OF STUDENT EXERCISES AND ACTIVITIES

Examining the Story

Students examine how another student became aware of the role of learning strengths in academic achievement and how she was able to identify and capitalize on her natural talents.

Students evaluate the protagonist's school-related attitudes and behavior, and they make predictions about the consequences of these behaviors and attitudes.

Identifying Your Own Learning Preferences

Students complete a **Personal Learning Modality Inventory**, which is designed to help them identify how they prefer to learn. After they complete the inventory, they interpret their responses using the guide provided in the unit.

Using Different Learning Modalities

Students examine the distinctive characteristics of the different types of learning modalities and review tips about how to apply these preferences. They then indicate how they might use these strengths and preferences when actually studying for a test.

Figuring Out Your Intelligence Type

Students examine the different intelligence types and expand on a list of specific careers in which the intelligence type might be a distinct asset.

Taking Stock

Students summarize in their own words what they've learned about their own learning strengths, preferred learning modality or modalities, and distinctive intelligence type.

Unit 1

Figuring Out How Students Learn Best

For Students

GETTING THE MOST OUT OF WHAT YOU'VE GOT

History was not Brittany's favorite subject, and the sixteen-year-old felt apprehensive about the history exam she had to take on Friday. The test would cover the French Revolution unit that the class had just completed. Brittany's anxiety was well founded. There was a ton of information to learn. Key facts and dates had to be flagged and memorized, and important historical concepts had to be understood and assimilated.

Brittany knew that the test was certain to be difficult. Her teacher had a well-earned reputation for giving tough exams, and she didn't hesitate to flunk kids who hadn't learned the material. Because Brittany was planning on going to college, grades were important to her. She also realized that she would need a partial scholarship and financial aid to cover her tuition and living expenses. Currently carrying a GPA of 3.2 in her sophomore year, Brittany recognized that she would have to raise her GPA to a minimum of 3.5 by her senior year to have a shot at getting one of the scholarships offered to the children of state employees. Getting into the state university and earning a scholarship were essential to attaining her long-range goal of becoming an attorney.

After calculating her current grade in her history course, Brittany realized that she was barely carrying a B. If she could get an A or an A– on the next test and an A– on the final exam, she could get a B+ in the class. With a good grade on her term paper, she might even get an A– for the semester. Brittany was certainly motivated to get the A–, and she had no problem with working conscientiously. Actually being able to get a good grade on the looming history exam was another story, however, and she clearly had her work cut out for her.

Brittany's mother taught at the local community college, and with great reluctance, Brittany decided to ask her mother for suggestions about how to prepare for the test. Her decision to ask for advice represented a major shift in attitude. Brittany prided herself on being independent, and she rarely involved her mother in any school-related issues. Brittany, however, was also a pragmatist (practical), and she was willing to do whatever was necessary to improve her chances of getting an A– on the test, even if it involved asking her mom for advice. She decided that it couldn't hurt to at least discuss the situation with her and hear what her mom had to say.

After the dinner table had been cleared and her younger brother had gone up to his room to do his homework, Brittany went into the kitchen where her mother was loading dishes into the dishwasher. Brittany stood by the sink, and her mom looked at her inquisitively.

Brittany: Mom, I have this big history test on Friday, and I really want to do well on it. The test will cover the French Revolution, which is actually quite interesting. But there's just so much to learn, and I'm feeling overwhelmed. I read the unit. I have my class notes, and I took textbook notes. But I know that I really don't know the information, and my teacher gives really tough tests. I barely got a B on the last unit test.

Mom: You know, of course, that I teach two sections of a study skills class that all first-year college students are required to take. One of the initial procedures in this course involves helping students to identify their learning strengths, learning preferences, and distinctive intelligence type.

Brittany: What does that mean?

Mom: Each person has different natural abilities. Some students prefer to learn visually, and others prefer to use the auditory channel. For example, a visual learner would rely on her notes and would prefer to assimilate information that's written down. An auditory learner would prefer to hear information and might use a tape recorder to help her learn. She would play the information over and over and just listen. Other students who are called tactile learners prefer to learn by actually touching, building, and drawing. Kinesthetic learners prefer to learn through movement. They can quickly learn complex basketball plays or cheerleading routines by practicing them. There are actually more than a half a dozen ways to learn. Smart students who identify their own learning strengths and preferences have a big advantage over those who don't have a clue about how they learn best. In addition to having learning strengths and learning preferences, students also have one or more distinctive types of intelligence. For example, some kids have mathematical intelligence. Others have musical intelligence or artistic intelligence. Others have athletic intelligence. There are actually nine intelligence types. The more you know about yourself and your abilities and the more you know about how you learn best, the better you'll do in school. You can gear your study procedures to your strengths, and you can learn how to use your strengths to compensate for your weaknesses.

Brittany: How do you identify the way you learn best, and how do you identify your intelligence type?

Mom: In the textbook for my course, there's a Personal Learning Modality Inventory. You could use it to help you identify how you prefer to learn. I have all of my students fill out this inventory on the first day of class. Would you like me to go upstairs and get you a copy?

Brittany: Definitely.

Mom: Of course, once you identify how you prefer to learn and how you learn best, you need to develop a practical strategy to capitalize on your strengths. There are many components involved in studying productively. You must identify the important information. You must make certain that you understand the important concepts. You must be able to memorize key facts and data. You must figure out what your teacher wants you to learn, and you must anticipate the questions that are likely to be asked on a test. The Personal Learning Modality Inventory is a good starting point.

After completing the checklist and analyzing her responses to the statements, Brittany concluded that she was primarily a visual learner. She needed to see information on paper to learn it. This explained why she liked to see information represented in graphs and diagrams and why she felt secure when she took very detailed notes in class.

Brittany's mom then showed her how to profit from her preferred learning modality. She encouraged her to put key facts and concepts on index cards so that she could review them easily, and she showed Brittany a technique for forming and imprinting visual pictures in her mind of what she was learning. She also showed Brittany how to make timelines of key historical events and how to commit these to memory. [*Please note:* All of these learning skills will be examined in later units.]

Brittany was glad that she hadn't been too proud to ask her mom for advice. In fact, to her great surprise, she actually found it fun to work with her mom, and she decided to use all of her suggestions. To her great relief, she received the A– she wanted on the test.

EXAMINING THE STORY

Brittany is clearly concerned about the history test has to take on Friday. Go back into the story and underline each of the reasons for her concerns. (For example: "There was so much information to learn.") You should be able to identify a minimum of three additional factors.

Now double-underline each suggestion that Brittany's mom made about steps Brittany could take to improve her chances of doing well on the test. You should be able to find nine. (Hint: Three steps are found in one sentence.) Then triple-underline each of Brittany's attitudes and behavior that you believe offer insight into her personality and values. (For example: "Grades were important to Brittany.") You should be able to identify a minimum of six additional school-related attitudes and behaviors that could affect her academic performance.

In the spaces that follow, write down each of Brittany's school-related attitudes and behaviors.

1. _____

How would you evaluate this behavior or attitude?

1	2	3	4	5	6	7	8	9	10
Not Smart			**Fairly Smart**				**Very Smart**		

2. _____

How would you evaluate this behavior or attitude?

1	2	3	4	5	6	7	8	9	10
Not Smart			**Fairly Smart**				**Very Smart**		

3. _____

How would you evaluate this behavior or attitude?

1	2	3	4	5	6	7	8	9	10
Not Smart			**Fairly Smart**				**Very Smart**		

4. _____

How would you evaluate this behavior or attitude?

1	2	3	4	5	6	7	8	9	10
Not Smart			**Fairly Smart**				**Very Smart**		

5. _____

How would you evaluate this behavior or attitude?

1	2	3	4	5	6	7	8	9	10
Not Smart			**Fairly Smart**				**Very Smart**		

6. _____

How would you evaluate this behavior or attitude?

1	2	3	4	5	6	7	8	9	10
Not Smart			**Fairly Smart**				**Very Smart**		

Based on what you read in the story, make three predictions about the consequences of Brittany's behaviors or attitudes. Circle whether you feel your predictions are **possible** or **probable.**

1. _____

       Possible   Probable

2. _____

       Possible   Probable

3. _____

       Possible   Probable

IDENTIFYING YOUR OWN
LEARNING PREFERENCES

As you read about Brittany's desire to identify her distinctive intelligence type, learning strengths, and learning preferences, you may be equally intrigued about identifying your own learning profile.

The following inventory will help you figure out how you learn best. Take a few minutes to complete it. At the end of the inventory, you'll find information that will help you to identify your preferred learning modality. You'll also find a description of each learning modality and tips on how best to use your natural abilities.

PERSONAL LEARNING MODALITY INVENTORY

	Yes	No	Not Sure
1. I learn best by reading information in textbooks, textbook notes, and lecture notes.	___	___	___
2. I can recall and understand information best when I can look at it.	___	___	___
3. Seeing a science experiment or a class demonstration helps me understand and learn the information.	___	___	___
4. I can remember information better when it's in diagrams, graphs, charts, and pictures.	___	___	___
5. When I can see information, it increases my interest, motivation, and involvement in what I am learning.	___	___	___
6. I learn best by listening to lectures, audiotapes, and spoken explanations.	___	___	___
7. I can understand and remember information better when I hear it.	___	___	___
8. Class discussions help me understand and learn what's being taught.	___	___	___
9. I can remember jokes and the words in songs when I hear them.	___	___	___
10. Hearing information that I'm expected to learn stimulates my interest, motivation, and active involvement.	___	___	___
11. I learn best when activities are physical.	___	___	___
12. I can recall and understand information better when I can move things around.	___	___	___
13. Doing experiment, drawing pictures, plotting graphs, making diagrams, or building models helps me understand what's being taught.	___	___	___

	Yes	No	Not Sure
14. I can usually learn the steps to a dance or athletic plays by practicing them once.	___	___	___
15. Physical activities stimulate my interest, motivation, and involvement in what I am learning.	___	___	___
16. I learn best when I am touching, holding, or manipulating what I need to learn.	___	___	___
17. I can put something together without instructions.	___	___	___
18. I can understand and recall how things work by handling them.	___	___	___
19. I enjoy mechanical projects, and I can disassemble and reassemble objects with little difficulty.	___	___	___
20. Hands-on activities stimulate my interest, motivation, and active involvement in what I am learning.	___	___	___
21. I like to learn by figuring out how to do something on my own.	___	___	___
22. I enjoy learning through trial and error.	___	___	___
23. I don't like to follow written or verbal instructions.	___	___	___
24. If I make a mistake, I learn from it and make adjustment so I can get it right the next time.	___	___	___
25. I like to work independently.	___	___	___

Interpreting the Survey:

Statements 1–5: These statements relate to visual learning. If you've responded primarily "Yes" to these statements, your learning preference is probably visual.

Statements 6–10: These statements relate to auditory learning. If you've responded primarily "Yes" to these statements, your learning preference is probably auditory.

Statements 11–15: These statements relate to kinesthetic learning. If you've responded primarily "Yes" to these statements, your learning preference is probably kinesthetic.

Statements 16–20: These statements relate to tactile learning. If you've responded primarily "Yes" to these statements, your learning preference is probably tactile.

Statements 21–25: These statements relate to experiential learning. If you've responded primarily "Yes" to these statements, your learning preference is probably experiential.

Please note: If you've answered "not sure" to many of the statements, don't be discouraged. Over the next few weeks, make a point of being conscious of how you learn and which modality or modalities are most comfortable and produce the best learning results. It's also possible to have more than one preferred modality and for you to prefer using one modality when learning certain information and another modality when learning other content.

USING DIFFERENT LEARNING MODALITIES

Auditory Learners assimilate information best by hearing it.

Characteristics: Auditory learners have an easier time understanding and remembering spoken information. They have an advantage in conversation-oriented foreign language classes because they can recall spoken dialogues, idiomatic expressions, vocabulary, grammar, and verb conjugations. They enjoy class discussions and participating in study groups and debating issues. They can remember the words to songs they hear as well as spoken details.

Tips for studying and learning productively:

- Recite information aloud.
- Focus intently on what the teacher says during lectures and class discussions.
- Deliberately create mental "audiotapes" of the key information. (You could include the information you need to learn in a favorite song that you hear in your mind and use the rhythm and the beat of the music to help you recall the data.)

Application:

If auditory learning is your strength and preferred learning modality, describe how you might use this natural talent to learn twenty new vocabulary words for an English test.

_____

_____

_____

_____

Visual Learners assimilate information best by seeing it.

Characteristics: Visual learners have the ability to understand and recall written information. They tend to excel in classes in which they're required to learn lots of data that's written in textbooks and recorded in their class notes. They're generally good spellers because they can *see* the correct spelling of words in their mind, and when they proofread, they can catch many of their own misspellings because words "don't *look* right." They're also good at remembering written telephone numbers, math facts, directions, data in diagrams and graphs, and people's faces.

Tips for studying and learning productively:

- Read and reread content written in textbooks and notes.
- Close your eyes and deliberately imprint visual information in your brain like a camera.
- Imprint an image on film or digitally.
- Use diagrams, illustrations, graphs, charts, and flashcards as study tools.

Application:

If visual learning is your strength and preferred learning modality, describe how you might use this natural talent to learn twenty new vocabulary words for an English test.

_____

_____

_____

_____

Tactile Learners assimilate information best by touching and manipulating materials.

Characteristics: Tactile learners learn most effectively when they are able to handle objects. They enjoy doing lab experiments. They like to sort and classify objects, repair cars, do construction projects, cook, and design and build models. They might use a skeleton in a biology class to help them learn the bones in the body or use a model of an atom to understand the way in which the nucleus is bound to and interacts with the electrons.

Tips for maximizing studying and learning effectiveness:

- Assimilate information whenever possible through hands-on manipulation of materials.
- Translate data into concrete representations (for example, build or draw something that incorporates the information you need to learn).

Application:

If tactile learning is your strength and preferred learning modality, describe how you might use this natural talent to learn facts in a science class.

_____

_____

_____

_____

Kinesthetic Learners assimilate information best by linking the data with movement.

Characteristics: Kinesthetic learners excel in activities that involve physical movement. They recall and understand information best when they involve their body in the learning process. They learn football plays by running them. They learn how to swing a golf club, make a layup, or put topspin on a tennis ball through hands-on experience, practice, and repetition.

Tips for maximizing studying and learning effectiveness:

- Assimilate information through movement whenever possible.
- Do "walk-throughs" and "run-throughs" to learn techniques, routines, and procedures.
- Incorporate physical movements to master academic content. (For example, tap out the beat of a poem to help learn what iambic pentameter means or create a movement pattern such as jumping rope to help learn facts in a history or science textbook.)

Application:

If kinesthetic learning is your strength and preferred learning modality, describe how you might use this natural talent to learn math or chemistry formulas.

_____

_____

_____

_____

Experiential Learners assimilate information best through active participation.

Characteristics: Experiential learners excel when they are involved in hands-on learning and share key learning characteristics with tactile learners and kinesthetic learners. They enjoy experimenting and deliberately learn from both their positive and negative experiences. Learning as they go along, they might begin to assemble something looking at the instructions. They do well in classes that involve working in a lab or using a workbench. Whenever possible, they try to make written or spoken information more concrete. This allows them to understand and remember information more readily.

Tips for maximizing studying and learning effectiveness:

- Assimilate information whenever possible through experimentation and trial and error.
- Combine experiential learning with tactile and kinesthetic learning (for example, take something apart to figure out how the pieces fit together).
- Deliberately apply what you're learning. (For example, practice a foreign language by speaking with native speakers, give "pretend" lectures to an imaginary class about something you need to learn, or figure out how to use a new software program by experimenting with it.)

Application:

If experiential learning is your strength and preferred learning modality, describe how you might use this natural talent to study for a history test.

_____

_____

_____

_____

FIGURING OUT YOUR INTELLIGENCE TYPE

Based on their performance in school, students often reach conclusions about their capabilities. If their grades are good, they're likely to conclude that they're bright. If their grades are poor, they're likely to conclude that they're not very bright. These conclusions about intelligence based on personal experiences in school may be inaccurate.

It's true that certain types of intelligence can help students do well in school, but other types of intelligence are equally valuable and yet do not always translate into A's in academic subjects. A Harvard professor named Howard Gardner concluded that the ways in which intelligence is traditionally defined and measured are inadequate and do not adequately validate the different types of human intelligence. Gardner identified nine types of natural intelligence, which he calls *Multiple Intelligences.* He contends that gifted athletes, musicians, actors, and dancers can be as brilliant in their area of expertise as physicists or mathematicians are in theirs.

To help you better understand your own distinctive type of intelligence, review the following descriptions. You may be surprised to learn that you're far more capable than you ever believed!

Types of Intelligence

- **Visual/Spatial Intelligence:** If you possess this type of intelligence, you have the ability to create images on paper and in your mind. Because you can naturally relate to and mentally imprint visual information, you prefer to learn by reading books and by viewing charts, demonstrations, videos, maps, and movies. You typically do well on tests that emphasize the recall of the written data in textbooks and class notes. Students with superior *visual/spatial intelligence* are usually *visual learners*. Those who capitalize on their natural visual/spatial intelligence often gravitate toward careers in areas such as engineering, mechanics, medicine, interior design, graphic arts, fine art, scholarly research, or architecture.

Application: Can you think of any other fields in which people might use visual/spatial intelligence to their advantage?

_____

_____

- **Verbal/Linguistic Intelligence:** If you posses this type of intelligence, you have good auditory and verbal skills, and you rely on spoken language to help you comprehend and retain information. You excel in classes that emphasize class discussions, oral presentations, study groups, and debates. You probably enjoy writing, telling stories, and expressing your conclusions and insights. Students with superior *verbal/linguistic intelligence* are usually *auditory learners.* Those who capitalize on their natural verbal/linguistic intelligence often gravitate toward careers in areas such as law, writing, journalism, acting, teaching, or politics.

Application: Can you think of any other fields in which people might use verbal/linguistic intelligence to their advantage?

_____

_____

- **Logical/Mathematical Intelligence:** If you possess this type of intelligence, you feel comfortable and capable when applying logic and reason. You tend to be more rational than emotional, and you have a questioning mind. You enjoy solving problems, doing puzzles, and figuring out "brain teasers." You think about concepts and ideas and can combine pieces of information to form a whole. You enjoy classifying and categorizing, doing calculations, and thinking about abstract ideas. You also enjoy doing experiments that help you better understand what's happening and the underlying issues. Students with superior *logical/mathematical intelligence* are usually *visual* and *experiential learners* as well.

Those who capitalize on their natural logical/mathematical intelligence often gravitate toward careers in areas such as mathematics, engineering, mechanics, geology, astronomy, theoretical science, physical sciences, scientific research, teaching, medicine, computer hardware and software development, programming, or accounting.

Application: Can you think of any other fields in which people might use logical/mathematical intelligence to their advantage?

_____

_____

- **Interpersonal Intelligence:** If you possess this type of intelligence, you're comfortable in social situations. You enjoy people, try to see issues from another person's perspective, and are sensitive to what others think and feel. You find it easy to establish relationships, organize events, mobilize people to work toward a common goal, resolve conflicts, build trust, maintain harmony, and encourage cooperation. Students with superior *interpersonal intelligence* may prefer to learn using any of the five learning modalities (auditory, visual, tactile, kinesthetic, experiential). Those who capitalize on their natural interpersonal intelligence often gravitate toward careers in areas such as sales, marketing, human resource development, management, advertising, psychology and counseling, or politics.

Application: Can you think of any other fields in which people might use interpersonal intelligence to their advantage?

_____

_____

- **Intrapersonal Intelligence:** If you possess this type of intelligence, you're probably introspective and aware of your feelings and those of other people. You're interested in understanding yourself, your friends, and the dynamics of your relationships. Students with superior intrapersonal intelligence may prefer to learn using any of the five listed learning modalities (auditory, visual, tactile, kinesthetic, experiential). Those who capitalize on their natural intrapersonal intelligence often gravitate toward careers in areas such as psychology, counseling, writing, religion, or teaching.

Application: Can you think of any other fields in which people might use intrapersonal intelligence to their advantage?

_____

_____

- **Bodily/Kinesthetic Intelligence:** If you possess this type of intelligence, you're well coordinated and enjoy and excel in sports. You use physical movement to assimilate information, and you're good at mastering the complex routines involved in dance steps, karate kicks, or gymnastic. Students with superior *bodily/kinesthetic intelligence* are usually primarily *tactile/kinesthetic* and *experiential learners*. Those who capitalize on their natural bodily/kinesthetic intelligence often gravitate toward careers in areas such as dance, athletics, acting, martial arts, sculpture, choreography, or coaching.

Application: Can you think of any other fields in which people might use bodily/kinesthetic intelligence to their advantage?

_____

_____

- **Musical/Rhythmic Intelligence:** If you possess this type of intelligence, you have a natural talent for performing or composing music. You respond to and can remember rhythms, lyrics, melodies, and tonal patterns. You enjoy singing, playing musical instruments, performing on stage, marching in a band, and rehearsing. Adept at recalling melodies, the words to songs, and the notes in musical scores, you think in musical patterns and respond primarily to sounds. Students with superior *musical/rhythmic intelligence* may prefer to learn using any of the five listed learning modalities (auditory, visual, tactile, kinesthetic, experiential). Those who capitalize on their natural music/rhythmic intelligence often become singers, musicians, composers, conductors, disc jockeys, or record producers.

Application: Can you think of any other fields in which people might use musical/rhythmic intelligence to their advantage?

_____

_____

- **Naturalist Intelligence:** If you possess this type of intelligence, you enjoy interacting with animals, nature, and wildlife. You're interested in ecology, the environment, and the factors that affect rain forests, oceans, jungles, food chains, and species survival. Students with superior naturalist intelligence may prefer to learn using any of the five listed learning modalities (auditory, visual, tactile, kinesthetic, experiential). Those who capitalize on their naturalist intelligence often gravitate to careers in botany, biology, oceanography, conservation, zoology, ecology, veterinary medicine, zoo management, or forestry.

Application: Can you think of any other fields in which people might use naturalist intelligence to their advantage?

_____

_____

Just as you may possess more that one learning preference, you may also possess more than one type of intelligence. For example, consider a student with exceptional bodily/kinesthetic intelligence who is a talented athlete. She may also possess exceptional interpersonal intelligence. In high school, she may excel in competitive volleyball, basketball, and tennis, and in college, she may play varsity sports while majoring in political science. Upon completing college, she may seek an internship with a member of Congress with the ultimate goal of becoming a politician. She may also actively participate in individual and team sports whenever possible.

Students have different natural abilities and learn in different ways. Science may be easy for one student to master because she has good logical/mathematical intelligence, while her friend may do well in English because he has good verbal/linguistic intelligence. There's nothing fundamentally superior about mathematical/logical intelligence versus verbal/linguistic intelligence. The distinctive capabilities associated with each type of intelligence allow students to excel in particular areas. The same principle applies to vocations and professions. One career may favor a certain type of intelligence, while another favors a different type.

Basic Principles for Success

You need to know

- Who you are.
- What you do well.
- What you want.
- What you enjoy.
- How to use your strengths to compensate for your weaknesses.
- What you need to do to attain your goals.
- How to learn productively.

TAKING STOCK

In the space that follows, summarize what you've learned about yourself—your learning strengths, your preferred learning modality or modalities, and your intelligence type. Indicate how you might use this information to improve your performance in school and to help you select a vocation or career for which you are naturally suited.

_____

_____

_____

_____

_____

_____

_____

Part 2

Getting Organized

Unit 2

Managing Time and Developing a Study Schedule

For Teachers

Objectives

This unit shows students how to handle the clock effectively and how to develop a personal study plan. Students learn to estimate how much time they realistically require to complete their assignments and then integrate this key information into a functional homework schedule.

LESSON PLAN

1. Students read the introductory case study titled **Homework War**. They identify and evaluate each of the protagonist's behaviors and attitudes and predict the consequences.

2. In **Planning Ahead**, students estimate the protagonist's weekly study requirements.

3. **Creating a Study Schedule**: Applying insights derived from their analysis of the protagonist's study requirements, students estimate their

own weekly and daily study requirements and record these estimates. They then examine a nine-step procedure for developing a personal study schedule and inspect a "Sample Study Schedule." Using the sample as a model, students practice the nine-step process and create their own Weekly Schedule.

4. Students commit to a **Study Schedule Contract** and agree to specific guidelines for making modifications.

5. Students keep a record of their grades for a specified period of time to gauge the efficacy of their study schedule.

6. Students examine the issue of **Study Breaks** when doing homework. They're provided with a realistic study break formula that is examined during a class discussion.

STUDENT SELF-REGULATION

Academic achievement in high school requires that students be able to regulate themselves, manage their time effectively, and get their work completed on time. Those who fail to acquire functional planning and time management skills are typically scattered and frequently in crisis mode as they scurry to do their assignments and meet impending deadlines. These "time-challenged" students rarely work up to their full scholastic potential.

To work efficiently and productively, students must be able to

- Estimate accurately how much time they require to complete daily homework assignments.
- Estimate accurately how much time they require to prepare for tests.
- Apply "divide and conquer" principles and break down assignments into specific manageable components.
- Establish a logical sequence for completing immediate tasks.
- Develop a plan for completing long-range projects such as reports and term papers and incorporate their study requirements into a practical and functional schedule.
- Meet deadlines.

Some students intuitively figure out how to manage time. They register how long it takes to do a particular task, store these data in their mental computers, and use the information as a frame of reference when they're faced with similar assignments. As they progress through elementary school into middle school, their database of task-related time requirements expands. By the time they enter high school, they should be able to make accurate judgments about how much time they must allocate to complete each of their academic obligations.

For example, based on past experience, students may conclude that a typical math homework assignment requires approximately twenty-five minutes and that reading and taking notes on the ten textbook pages that their science teacher typically assigns requires approximately an hour. They realize that to study effectively for a social studies chapter test, they must allocate approximately four hours. From experience, they know that they can avoid a crisis in their English class if they allot three weeks to read a book for a monthly book report, read twenty minutes each evening, and set aside four hours to write the report. As students budget their time, they consider key factors such as the number of pages in the book, the degree of difficulty of the content, and their language arts skills. They must also factor into the equation how long it should take them to write a first draft, edit and polish the draft, prepare a final draft, and proof-read for spelling and grammatical errors. They may decide to schedule twenty minutes of reading time each school night for three weeks and allocate two or three sustained blocks of time for writing the report, or they may decide to schedule more time for reading during the weekends.

FACTORS THAT CONTRIBUTE TO INSUFFICIENT TIME AWARENESS

The ability to coordinate strategic planning and effective time management is a critically important academic achievement tool that many otherwise capable students may not acquire. The net effect of this planning and clock-handling deficiency is diminished performance that can undermine students' academic self-confidence, motivation, and effort.

Difficulty with planning and time management is particularly prevalent in underachieving students. To function productively in school, these students must be taught how to assess their obligations and make realistic time esti-mates of their study requirements that are based on their current skills.

For complex reasons, many students do not naturally acquire an apprecia-tion for time demands and constraints. The parents of these students may not be particularly time-attentive, or, paradoxically, they may actually be obses-sively time-attentive. Students may react by consciously or unconsciously rejecting behavior that they consider weird and stress-producing. Whatever the underlying causal factors, many potentially capable students may never imprint the fundamental cause-and-effect principle that they must first do *this* in order to achieve *that*.

Students with attention-deficit/hyperactivity disorder (ADHD) often have an especially difficult time managing the clock. Simply staying on task consumes much, if not all, of their physical and mental energy. In many cases, the most pressing concern for these students is to get the immediate tasks completed as quickly and painlessly as possible. Scheduling multifaceted projects and making predictions about time requirements often eclipses their self-discipline resources. Managing long-range projects such as a term paper or a book report can be over-whelming, and the common "solution" is to put off dealing with the project for as long as possible. This procrastination produces predictable consequences: incomplete assignments, missed deadlines, failure to study adequately for tests, chronic stress and anxiety, repeated crises, and lowered grades.

The demand for effective time management skills significantly increases in high school. Being required to handle assignments in five different subjects can cause some students to go into meltdown. Those who do melt down are typically in a continual crisis mode and often become overwhelmed, discouraged, demoralized, and academically dysfunctional. If these "time-challenged" students conclude that they can't handle their academic obligations, they may shut down academically. Others may compensate by becoming increasingly dependent on their parents to supervise them and help them complete their work.

Ironically, students with the greatest need to improve their time management skills are often the most resistant to doing so. Some are oblivious to the obvious consequences of inefficient time management. Others are in denial and don't want to confront the implications of their poor planning and disorganization.

All students, even those with ADHD, can be taught effective time management skills. The first step in the process is to show them how to define and prioritize their academic obligations and allocate sufficient time to meet those obligations. Those who require extra time to complete projects should be urged to build a buffer into their schedule. They must practice making "best guess" predictions of the time requirements based on a careful assessment of the particular task and past experience with similar tasks. If their predictions prove inaccurate, they must be taught how to analyze what went wrong and make adjustments in their future planning.

REINFORCING TIME-MANAGEMENT PROCEDURES

By incorporating short- and long-term planning and scheduling exercises as integral components of the curriculum, you can play a key role in helping students improve their ability to manage the clock. For example, students might plan a class project and design a schedule that requires careful time management. They could prioritize the steps needed to complete the task and estimate the time requirements for each step. These data could then be plotted into a flow chart. Miscalculations could be discussed and appropriate changes made. To reinforce basic time-management principles, every student might be required to develop a formal step-by-step schedule for completing a long-range project such as a term paper.

By showing students how to analyze challenges, break down projects and major assignments into manageable parts, and make realistic estimates about how much time must be allotted to complete each component of the project or assignment, you are tangibly reinforcing critically important clock-handling procedures. The reproducible components in this unit are specifically designed to achieve these objectives, and the exercises and activities provide ample opportunities for students to practice and apply basic time-management procedures.

To ensure mastery and assimilation of the basic time-management procedures taught in this unit, you can provide opportunities for additional reinforcement. For example, students might examine the steps and time requirements involved in preparing effectively for a midterm science exam or for writing a term paper. Based on their past experiences with studying and a realistic assessment of their own study efficiency, each student could then set up a personal schedule that allocates the time required to handle the challenge.

As is the case with mastering any skill, time-management competency will improve with repeated opportunities for practice. Once students perceive the value of managing their time more efficiently and experience the payoffs, they should be more receptive to incorporating these planning and scheduling skills into their daily modus operandi.

Behaviors Often Associated With Time-Management Problems

- Procrastination
- Irresponsibility
- Resistance to studying and doing homework
- Difficulty making accurate time estimates and projections
- Failure to allocate realistic amounts of time for studying, preparing for tests, completing assignments and projects, and proofreading
- Difficulty planning
- Disregard of cause-and-effect principles
- Excessive study interruptions
- Poor organization
- Dependency on others
- Inattention to details
- Failure to record assignments properly
- Failure to develop a study strategy
- Chronic stress and anxiety
- Incomplete assignments
- Missed deadlines

SUMMARY OF STUDENT EXERCISES AND ACTIVITIES

Examining the Story

Students practice linking cause-and-effect principles with time management and organization. The case study describes a student who is having difficulty managing her time and obligations and who is in conflict with her mother. Students analyze and assess Tanya's attitudes and behavior and jpredict the likely consequences.

Planning Ahead

Students learn and practice a step-by-step method for creating an efficient, effective, and personalized study plan. The activity introduces fundamental time-management principles. The goal is for students to arrive at a key insight: They can make their life easier by planning ahead.

The first step in designing a personal schedule is to estimate the amount of daily study time that's required in each subject to do a first-rate job. A class discussion that reinforces the principles and procedure would clearly be beneficial.

Creating a Study Schedule

Students are now ready to develop their own study schedule. They apply the methods introduced on pages 52–58. They carefully analyze their own daily study requirements in each subject, and they learn a nine-step procedure for creating a schedule that is tailored to their own needs. They then transfer their estimated average study requirements in each subject onto a study schedule. (Students who have difficulty following instructions may require additional help with this exercise.) It's suggested that you have extra copies of the Study Schedule available for students who make mistakes in coloring and coding their schedules.

A Study Schedule Contract

Once students produce a reasonable and practical study schedule, suggest that they try an experiment. Encourage them to sign a "contract" (they can create their own or use the model in the worksheet). By signing this contract, they agree to adhere to their study schedule for two weeks before making adjustments. The contract is intended to elicit a commitment from students to use their study schedule. The ultimate goal is for them to internalize the time-management and organizational principles. After two weeks, students should fine-tune their schedules and use these revised schedules for four additional weeks before making further changes.

By guiding students to the realization that schedules are not a diabolical adult conspiracy designed to make their life miserable, you can generally defuse "knee-jerk" resistance. Your goal is to help students realize that study schedules do not need to be restrictive, boring, or unfair and that a reasonable schedule will make their studying more efficient and produce more free time.

Study Breaks

The frequency and duration of study breaks can be an emotionally charged issue. Your students undoubtedly have divergent attitudes about the issue of study breaks, and they should be encouraged to express their views in an open, nonjudgmental context. Ideally, students will recognize that they must exert self-discipline if they are to study productively. During a class discussion, examine reasonable study break formulas. Urge students to experiment with their personal study break formula until they develop one that "works" for them.

Unit 2

Managing Time and Developing a Study Schedule

For Students

HOMEWORK WAR

Tanya prepared herself for the inevitable. She knew that as soon as her mother returned home from work, she would ask her if she had started her homework. It was the same ritual every day. If Tanya said she had completed her homework in school, her mother would look at her suspiciously and say, "Oh, really?" Tanya hated that. She would emphatically insist she had done all of her work and tell her mother to stop pestering her. Then her mother would say, "Well, I hope so because I really want to see better grades on your next report card."

Of course, when Tanya looked objectively at the situation, she had to admit that she could understand her mother's concern and suspicion. She was getting mainly C's and D's in school, and her teachers usually noted on her report card that she was not handing in all of her assignments and not studying adequately for tests.

Ever since elementary school, Tanya's teachers had commented that she was bright, but most had also complained that she was lazy. Her mother was convinced Tanya was capable of B's and A's, and she had told her daughter "thousands of times" that she was an underachiever.

Being stubborn, Tanya refused to make any changes in her attitude or study habits. She told her friends she didn't care about school and she found most of the work "dumb." She also told them she couldn't care less about her grades. When she finished school, she wanted to find a job, buy a car, and share an apartment with some of her friends. She did just enough work to pass her classes and little more.

When Tanya was in middle school, her mother used to punish her for bad grades by grounding her or taking away privileges. It didn't help, and Tanya actually took pride in the fact that her mother's strategy hadn't changed her attitude, behavior, or school performance.

Now that Tanya was in high school, her mother appeared more resigned to the situation. She had, however, told Tanya that if she didn't do better in school, she would not allow her to get her driver's license. This made Tanya very angry. She hadn't yet decided if the payoff of being allowed to drive was a sufficient enticement for her to get more serious about studying.

EXAMINING THE STORY

The daily conflict between Tanya and her mother about homework is predictable. In the story, it's clear that certain events happen every evening and in a certain order. This might be described as a *ritual*. A ritual is something that occurs over and over again in the same way.

Go back into the story and underline each event that would happen when Tanya returned from school. (For example: "Tanya prepared herself for the anticipated question.") Then number each underlined event in the order in which it happened.

Now double-underline all references to how Tanya's teachers and mother felt about her ability and performance. Then triple-underline each of Tanya's own attitudes and behaviors regarding her schoolwork. Underline specific behaviors and attitudes that describe **how she felt about school or homework.** (For example: "She told her friends she didn't care . . .")

In the spaces that follow write down each of Tanya's *attitudes*. Try to find at least *four.*

1. _____

How would you evaluate this behavior or attitude?

1	2	3	4	5	6	7	8	9	10
Not Smart			**Fairly Smart**				**Very Smart**		

2. _____

How would you evaluate this behavior or attitude?

1	2	3	4	5	6	7	8	9	10
Not Smart			**Fairly Smart**				**Very Smart**		

3. _____

How would you evaluate this behavior or attitude?

1	2	3	4	5	6	7	8	9	10
Not Smart			**Fairly Smart**				**Very Smart**		

4. _____

How would you evaluate this behavior or attitude?

1	2	3	4	5	6	7	8	9	10
Not Smart			**Fairly Smart**				**Very Smart**		

Make three predictions about the consequences of Tanya's behaviors or attitudes. Circle whether you feel your predictions are **possible** or **probable.**

1. _____

Possible   Probable

2. _____

Possible   Probable

3. _____

Possible   Probable

PLANNING AHEAD

You probably concluded from the description of Tanya's actions that she didn't have an effective study plan. Let's assume Tanya decides that she desperately wants to get her driver's license and realizes that to do so, she must improve her grades. Pretend that you're Tanya's friend and that you're a good student. Tanya asks you for specific ideas about how to get better grades, and you suggest she create a study strategy. You tell her that the first step in creating this plan is to list the subjects she is taking in school and to estimate how much time she realistically needs to spend every evening doing her homework and studying in each subject.

For the purposes of this exercise, assume that Tanya is taking *the same subjects you are.* Based on your own study experience, estimate the appropriate daily study and homework requirements for each subject. Use minutes instead of hours (for example: Math—forty-five minutes.)

Approximate Study Time Required Each School Night

Subjects:	*Study Time Required (in minutes):*
_____	_____
_____	_____
_____	_____
_____	_____
_____	_____
_____	_____

Approximate Total Minutes of Studying Each Evening: _____

Of course, Tanya's teachers may assign more homework than your teachers, or they may assign less. It's also possible that Tanya may require more time to complete her assignments than you do, or she may require less time. We'll assume, however, that your estimates based on your own experiences are accurate and would also apply to Tanya.

For example, let's say Tanya is taking Spanish II. Let's assume her teacher has indicated *when* the next test will be given and *which* specific regular and irregular verbs, vocabulary, and grammar rules she needs to learn for the test. If Tanya thinks strategically, she could create a focused study plan that will help her do well on the test. She might plan to learn a certain number of specific verb conjugations and vocabulary each night. She might decide to study twenty-five minutes on Monday, Tuesday, and Wednesday evenings. On Thursday, the night before the test, she might plan to spend forty-five minutes studying. She might also plan to review the assigned material in school with a friend who is doing well in Spanish. She and her friend might even make up a practice test.

If Tanya's math or science teacher assigns less homework on a particular evening, or if she gets her work done in school, she may not have to spend twenty-five minutes studying that subject. She could make reasonable adjustments in her schedule and devote the freed-up time to another subject. The schedule provides a general guideline, but it can vary from time to time.

Let's assume Tanya "turns over a new leaf" and follows your recommendations about a conscientious daily study schedule. Predict the likely consequences for the following items.

Her grades: _____

Her feelings about her improved school performance: _____

Her mother's reaction about her new study plan and improved academic achievement: _____

List other short- and long-term payoffs Tanya might derive from her new study plan:

1. _____

2. _____

3. _____

4. _____

CREATING A STUDY SCHEDULE

Before you create your own personal study schedule, examine the *sample schedule* that appears on page 55. As you can see, this **Study Schedule** indicates blocks of time between getting home from school every afternoon and going to bed each evening. The schedule divides time into half-hour units. At the bottom of the schedule is a code. The symbols represent how Tanya has decided to use each block of time. For example, one pattern represents time spent eating, and another represents free time. Instead of geometric designs, you might prefer to use colored pencils or felt pens.

There are clear advantages to planning how much time you need to set aside for homework and studying. If you create an effective personal study schedule and use it consistently, you'll discover that your grades have improved (assuming, of course, that you also use the specific study techniques you will learn in this book). With a study schedule, you'll also be able to block out free time to do things you enjoy. The secrets to getting good grades and having free time are to use your time efficiently and to study efficiently and effectively.

Steps for Creating a Study Schedule

Step 1: Write down all of the subjects you are taking and estimate the average number of *minutes* you need to spend **each day** in each subject. This may vary, of course, if a teacher doesn't assign any homework in a particular subject or if no tests or quizzes are to be given during the week. For planning purposes, however, you're interested in the average amount of study time required each day. (This schedule will probably be the same as the one you already completed on page 52.)

Subjects: *Average Study Time Required (minutes):*

_____   _____

_____   _____

_____   _____

_____   _____

_____   _____

_____   _____

Approximate Total Minutes of Studying Each Evening: _____

Step 2: Write down the times when you get home from school, have dinner, and go to bed. (Occasionally there may be changes, but list times that are usually consistent.)

Get home from school: _____

Dinner time: _____

Bed time: _____.

It's time to use this information to complete your schedule. Look at the schedule on page 56. It indicates the time between getting home from school each day and going to bed. Before attempting to complete your own schedule, read the following instructions and carefully examine Tanya's schedule on page 55, which represents how her schedule might look. Before filling in your schedule, plan how you want to use your time. If you make a mistake, ask your teacher for another copy of the blank schedule.

Step 3: Use different colored pencils or felt pens to indicate when you eat dinner and when you go to bed. If you eat between 6:00 and 6:30, color in that time every day in a color of your choice. For example, you might choose red for eating. If you eat between 6:00 and 6:45 color in one and one half strips. Below the schedule, fill in one of the little boxes with the selected color and write, "Dinner Time." Fill in a second box with a second color and write "Bed Time."

Step 4: Use a different color to indicate when you want to study and do homework. For example, you might get home from basketball practice at 5:00, and you may want to work from 5:30 to 6:00. Dinner might be from 6:00 to 6:45. You might want to have some time for yourself until 7:00 and then do your remaining homework until 10:00. (Remember to fill in the color code box below.) The rest of the evening until bedtime could be free time! You can do what you want—watch TV or call your friends. Of course, if you have a test to study for or a report that is due the next day, you may need to work beyond 10:00.

Step 5: Use a different color to indicate when you want to schedule free time. For example, if you get home from basketball practice at 5:00 and want to talk on the phone with your friends until 6:00, schedule this time in the color of your choice. Below the schedule fill in the little box with the color and write: "Free Time"

Step 6: Compare your completed schedule with those of your friends. You may want to make modifications.

Step 7: As an experiment, keep to your schedule for two weeks and see if your grades improve. (On page 57, you'll find a simple system for keeping track of your grades.)

TANYA'S SAMPLE WEEKLY SCHEDULE					
TIME:	**MONDAY**	**TUESDAY**	**WEDNESDAY**	**THURSDAY**	**FRIDAY**
3:30 - 4:00	×	×	×	×	×
4:00 - 4:30	×	×	×	×	×
4:30 - 5:00	×	×	×	×	×
5:00 - 5:30	×	×	×	×	×
5:30 - 6:00	0	0	0	0	0
6:00 - 6:30	+	+	+	+	+
6:30 - 7:00	0	0	0	0	0
7:00 - 7:30	*	*	*	*	*
7:30 - 8:00	*	*	*	*	*
8:00 - 8:30	*	*	*	*	*
8:30 - 9:00	*	*	*	*	*
9:00 - 9:30	0	0	0	0	0
9:30 - 10:00	*	*	*	*	*
10:00 - 10:30	*	*	*	*	*
10:30 - 11:00	z	z	z	z	z

CODE: [×] <u>Track</u>   [0] <u>Free Time</u>   [+] <u>Dinner</u>   [*] <u>Study</u>   [z] <u>Sleep</u>

Step 8: Critically evaluate and fine-tune your schedule after the two-week trial period. If appropriate, make changes to improve it. Remember, your schedule is your ally and not your enemy! You want it to serve you and work for you.

MY WEEKLY SCHEDULE					
TIME:	MONDAY	TUESDAY	WEDNESDAY	THURSDAY	FRIDAY
3:30 - 4:00					
4:00 - 4:30					
4:30 - 5:00					
5:00 - 5:30					
5:30 - 6:00					
6:00 - 6:30					
6:30 - 7:00					
7:00 - 7:30					
7:30 - 8:00					
8:00 - 8:30					
8:30 - 9:00					
9:00 - 9:30					
9:30 - 10:00					
10:00 - 10:30					
10:30 - 11:00					

CODE: [ ] _____   [ ] _____   [ ] _____   [ ] _____   [ ] _____

Step 9: Use the grade-tracking form on page 57 to record your grades in every subject (tests, essays, reports, etc.) once you begin using your study schedule. Do this for the two-week trial period before you fine-tune your schedule. This recording process will allow you to track your performance and help you make adjustments. If, for example, your math grade doesn't improve, or even goes down, you'll need to schedule more time for doing math homework and studying for tests.

Once you work out the kinks in your study schedule and your schedule demonstrates that it's working, you'll probably discover you have a lot more free time. The key is to maintain the schedule even if it's occasionally inconvenient or requires sacrifices. Make changes only when absolutely necessary. For example, if your parents want you to go out for dinner with them on a particular evening, you'll obviously have to make changes in your schedule that night. (It's also recommended that you create a weekend study schedule.)

Having a schedule is like beginning a training program in a sport. If you're on the track team and want to improve your time in the 100 meters, you have to discipline yourself. You also have to maintain your training schedule. In school, this commitment means starting your homework when indicated on your schedule even if there's something else you would rather be doing. This can be a challenge. You might be talking with friends after school, and you realize it's 5:30, the time *you* decided to begin studying. Saying to your friends, "I have to go home and do my homework" will be difficult. You'll have to remind yourself that you made a commitment because you realized that doing so was *smart* and *strategic.* You'll keep your commitment because you recognize that it's more important than being with your friends. You can always talk to them later. Self-discipline requires *less* discipline when you're doing something you want to do! When you are doing what you want to do, you're not answering to anyone but yourself.

Keeping Track of Your Performance

SUBJECT: _____

Homework:	Date ____ Grade ____	Date ____ Grade ____	Date ____ Grade ____
	Date ____ Grade ____	Date ____ Grade ____	Date ____ Grade ____
	Date ____ Grade ____	Date ____ Grade ____	Date ____ Grade ____
	Date ____ Grade ____	Date ____ Grade ____	Date ____ Grade ____
Tests:	Date ____ Grade ____	Date ____ Grade ____	Date ____ Grade ____
	Date ____ Grade ____	Date ____ Grade ____	Date ____ Grade ____
Reports/Papers:	Date ____ Grade ____	Date ____ Grade ____	Date ____ Grade ____
	Date ____ Grade ____	Date ____ Grade ____	Date ____ Grade ____

SUBJECT: _____

Homework:	Date ____ Grade ____	Date ____ Grade ____	Date ____ Grade ____
	Date ____ Grade ____	Date ____ Grade ____	Date ____ Grade ____
	Date ____ Grade ____	Date ____ Grade ____	Date ____ Grade ____
	Date ____ Grade ____	Date ____ Grade ____	Date ____ Grade ____
Tests:	Date ____ Grade ____	Date ____ Grade ____	Date ____ Grade ____
	Date ____ Grade ____	Date ____ Grade ____	Date ____ Grade ____
Reports/Papers:	Date ____ Grade ____	Date ____ Grade ____	Date ____ Grade ____
	Date ____ Grade ____	Date ____ Grade ____	Date ____ Grade ____

SUBJECT: _____

Homework: Date ____ Grade ____   Date ____ Grade ____   Date ____ Grade ____

Date ____ Grade ____   Date ____ Grade ____   Date ____ Grade ____

Date ____ Grade ____   Date ____ Grade ____   Date ____ Grade ____

Date ____ Grade ____   Date ____ Grade ____   Date ____ Grade ____

Tests: Date ____ Grade ____   Date ____ Grade ____   Date ____ Grade ____

Date ____ Grade ____   Date ____ Grade ____   Date ____ Grade ____

Reports/Papers: Date ____ Grade ____   Date ____ Grade ____   Date ____ Grade ____

Date ____ Grade ____   Date ____ Grade ____   Date ____ Grade ____

SUBJECT: _____

Homework: Date ____ Grade ____   Date ____ Grade ____   Date ____ Grade ____

Date ____ Grade ____   Date ____ Grade ____   Date ____ Grade ____

Date ____ Grade ____   Date ____ Grade ____   Date ____ Grade ____

Date ____ Grade ____   Date ____ Grade ____   Date ____ Grade ____

Tests: Date ____ Grade ____   Date ____ Grade ____   Date ____ Grade ____

Date ____ Grade ____   Date ____ Grade ____   Date ____ Grade ____

Reports/Papers: Date ____ Grade ____   Date ____ Grade ____   Date ____ Grade ____

Date ____ Grade ____   Date ____ Grade ____   Date ____ Grade ____

SUBJECT: _____

Homework: Date ____ Grade ____   Date ____ Grade ____   Date ____ Grade ____

Date ____ Grade ____   Date ____ Grade ____   Date ____ Grade ____

Date ____ Grade ____   Date ____ Grade ____   Date ____ Grade ____

Date ____ Grade ____   Date ____ Grade ____   Date ____ Grade ____

Tests: Date ____ Grade ____   Date ____ Grade ____   Date ____ Grade ____

Date ____ Grade ____   Date ____ Grade ____   Date ____ Grade ____

Reports/Papers: Date ____ Grade ____   Date ____ Grade ____   Date ____ Grade ____

Date ____ Grade ____   Date ____ Grade ____   Date ____ Grade ____

A STUDY SCHEDULE CONTRACT

Training schedules for athletes (example: run three miles every day during the off season, and do 100 sit-ups and 200 push-ups) and New Year's Resolutions (example: cut back on sweets) are often hard to keep. There can be a powerful temptation when it's raining or when you have a slight sore throat or headache to "let things slide." The following day, you may be tempted to let things slide again. It gets easier and easier to rationalize not working out. Before long, you abandon the schedule or resolution altogether.

As an experiment, create a personal "contract" (or use the sample contract that follows) to help you keep to your schedule. This contract is an agreement between *you* and *yourself.* Remember, keeping your commitments is an important part of thinking smart and improving your grades!

Study Contract Between Me and Myself

Date: _____

To Me: (write your name)

I, _____, agree to use my study schedule for a two-week trial period. If after using the schedule for two weeks I decide that my schedule should be changed or fine-tuned, I will do so. Once I make these changes, I agree to use the revised schedule for a minimum of four weeks. If I'm pleased with the results and my grades improve, I'll continue to use the schedule for the rest of the school year, making changes and adjustments every four weeks. Finally, I agree to keep to my schedule without having to be prodded or reminded by my parents.

Signed: ___._____

Witnesses (Optional): _____

STUDY BREAKS

No one can study without taking breaks. Taking a break, however, does not mean getting up every ten minutes to call a friend, play with your dog, talk with your brother, or watch TV.

Successful students who think strategically recognize the value of concentrating when they study. They discipline themselves to work for a set period of time before taking time out to "recharge their batteries."

A Suggested Formula for Study Breaks
**Study a minimum of twenty-five minutes
before taking a five-minute break**

Some students can concentrate for longer periods and may prefer to study for thirty to fifty minutes before resting. If you can't work for twenty-five minutes at a stretch, consider creating a *personal training program* to build

---

up your study stamina. You might use an egg timer. Before beginning to study, set the timer for ten minutes. When the buzzer goes off, take a five-minute rest. The next day, set the timer at eleven minutes. Each day add one minute before taking your break. Soon you'll be able to study for twenty-five minutes or longer without any difficulty.

Too many study breaks are distracting. Training and disciplining your brain is like training and disciplining your body for sports. Desire, practice, and commitment produce strength, endurance, achievement, and excellence. These same qualities also produce improved grades.

Unit 3

Recording and Organizing Assignments

For Teachers

Objectives

This unit presents a simple and practical system for recording assignments and provides opportunities for students to practice and master these procedures. The unit also examines how to utilize teacher-prepared assignment handouts most effectively.

LESSON PLAN

1. Students read the introductory case study and underline each of Rebecca's behaviors and attitudes about recording her assignments. They describe each behavior or attitude in their own words, evaluate it, and predict the potential consequence. They then follow the same procedure with Matthew's behaviors and attitudes. After completing the exercise, students discuss their evaluations and rationales.

2. Students examine a **Sample Assignment Sheet.** Using this sample as a model, they transfer a hypothetical assignment to a **Practice Assignment Sheet.** They then discuss and compare their work.

61

3. In **Practice Writing Down Assignments,** students record a more extensive assignment. The activity demonstrates that the procedure is easy and effective and can quickly become a habit. Before students begin the worksheet, a list of basic abbreviations that save time and space is introduced. This list can, of course, be expanded, and students should be encouraged to create their own comprehensible abbreviations.

4. Once students have learned the assignment-recording system, they must practice the procedure to achieve mastery. Hand out several copies of the assignment sheet, and have students use the sheets to record their actual weekly assignments in all subjects. After completing the week-long experiment, the class should discuss the benefits (or possible drawbacks) of the system. Encourage students to fine-tune the procedures. If feasible, examine each student's assignment sheet and provide feedback and suggestions.

5. In **Teacher-Prepared Assignment Handouts,** students learn a simple method for identifying and highlighting instructions and details that are vital to their being able to complete their homework as directed.

THINKING ABOUT HOMEWORK DETAILS

Inattentiveness to details is a common behavioral characteristic of students with poor study skills. This negligence is often particularly prevalent when students are recording their homework assignments. Many underachieving students have never developed an effective homework-recording system. Others refuse to copy down the vital information and details that are essential to doing their work properly. These students may delude themselves into thinking that they can remember what their teachers have assigned and when the work is due, or they may simply be apathetic about doing their homework and meeting deadlines.

Students who are chronically nonchalant about recording their assignments often

- Hand in work that does not conform to their teachers' explicit instructions.
- "Forget" to do assigned work.
- "Forget" to study for tests.
- Submit incomplete work.
- Miss deadlines.
- Study passively and ineffectually.
- Receive lower grades.

The performance implications of maladaptive homework-recording behaviors are predictable and include diminished performance and academic self-confidence. It's axiomatic that students who don't know what their assignments are and when they're due are on a collision course with the grading system.

Some students develop an effective system for recording and organizing their homework without formal instruction. Other students lack these intuitive skills. These students require methodical instruction in how to write down their assignments, and they require repeated opportunities to practice the procedures under teacher supervision. Fortunately, basic homework-recording methods can be quickly and easily taught and mastered.

You may be thinking that homework-recording instruction is unnecessary for your students because you prepare and distribute weekly assignment sheets. Other teachers, however, may not be as accommodating as you are, and they may require their students to take responsibility for recording the information that is posted on the chalkboard or announced orally at the end of each class. (*Please note:* The last activity in this unit provides practical guidelines for using teacher-prepared assignment sheets.)

Imagine that a teacher writes the following assignment on the chalkboard:

History Assignment

Read Unit 3, pages 64–85. Answer questions on page 86. Do even-numbered questions (#'s 2, 4, 6, and 8). Complete sentences. Skip line between each answer. Write your name next to the red margin on the top line and write the date below it. Due tomorrow.

Some students will be convinced that they can remember the assignment without having to record it. Others may simply write down, "Unit 3, Do exercises." Having omitted key information, their work is unlikely to conform to the teacher's explicit instructions.

By providing your students with clear, easy-to-follow guidelines for recording homework, you are furnishing them with a tool that's critically important to academic achievement. Once they master a practical and effective homework-recording system and experience its payoffs, they'll be far more likely to use the system voluntarily.

SUMMARY OF STUDENT EXERCISES AND ACTIVITIES

Examining the Story

Students examine, evaluate, and contrast the attitudes and behavior of two very different students. The objective of this exercise is to motivate students to evaluate their own homework-recording method and to help them appreciate two key academic cause-and-effect principles: (1) By functioning efficiently, they can improve their school performance, and (2) by functioning inefficiently, they will diminish their performance.

Students identify and evaluate each of Rebecca's productive behaviors and attitudes and make predictions about the consequences. They then identify and evaluate each of Matthew's counterproductive behaviors and attitudes and make predictions about the consequences.

A System for Recording Assignments: Recording an Assignment and Practicing Writing Down Recording Assignments

These exercises provide hands-on practice. Students record a facsimile assignment on a Practice Assignment Sheet. (Some students may need extra guidance, monitoring, and feedback during this procedure.) Encourage the use of shorthand and abbreviations, but emphasize that they must include vital information and be able to decipher what they write.

Using the Sample Assignment Sheet as a guide, students practice recording a facsimile of a typical week's assignments on a Practice Assignment Sheet. This exercise is designed to reinforce mastery of the requisite procedures. With practice and guidance, most students will quickly become adept at recording their assignments properly. The goal is for them to make this process an automatic habit.

Using Your Assignment Sheet and Using Teacher-Prepared Assignment Handouts

Students are now ready to use the assignment-recording system in their classes. Periodic supervision to ensure they are using the system may be appropriate, especially in the case of chronically disorganized students.

Launching Your Homework-Recording System

Students are encouraged to evaluate the efficacy of the Study Max homework-recording system and to compare it objectively with any other system that they may have been using. They then examine how to use a weekly assignments handout productively, and they learn how different-colored highlight pens can be used to flag key details, due dates, and long-range assignments.

Unit 3

Recording and Organizing Assignments

For Students

THE RECORDING ASSIGNMENTS BLUES

All the students in Spanish 2 knew that their teacher was infamous for assigning lots of homework and giving difficult tests. Ms. Ramirez was a great teacher, but she also had a well-earned reputation for being a tough grader, and kids would often groan when they learned that they had been assigned to her class. They realized that they would have their work cut out for them.

Ms. Ramirez began to write the homework assignment on the chalkboard. "Thurs.: Test: Chap. 3. Know irregular verbs, vocabulary, idiomatic expressions, and present tense subjunctive of all assigned -ir, -er, and -ar regular verbs." As she wrote down the assignment, Ms. Ramirez gave clues about what the test would cover. For example, she told students that they should know which phrases always required the subjective tense, and they needed to learn all of the new vocabulary words in the chapter and be able to use them in a sentence that clearly indicated that they understood the definitions.

Rebecca transferred the information about the test from the board to her assignment sheet. She also wrote down the teacher's verbal clues. She was determined to get at least a B+ on the test, and she planned to use the clues to help her prepare.

While Ms. Ramirez had her back to the class and was writing the assignment on the board, Matthew was drawing racecars in his binder. He was taking the Spanish class because his parents insisted that he do so, but he had absolutely no interest in learning the language. In fact, Matthew really didn't care about any of his subjects. He felt like a prisoner in school. What he really wanted to do was buy a car, fix it up, and spend the day driving around town.

After Matthew finished his drawing of the new Corvette, he turned to an empty page in his binder and scribbled "Spanish test." He then reached furtively into his backpack for his *Car and Driver* magazine, and he surreptitiously placed it in his binder. After glancing at Ms. Ramirez to make certain that she hadn't seen this sleight of hand, Matthew began to read about the new 360-horsepower Cobra.

Matthew thought that if he was lucky, he could get a C– or a D on the test, and that was perfectly OK with him. He planned to review the chapter on the way to school on Thursday.

EXAMINING THE STORY

Carefully reread the case study. Underline each of Rebecca's specific behaviors (what she actually did) when Ms. Ramirez announced the Spanish test and double-underline each of her attitudes (what she was thinking).

Write down each of Rebecca's **behaviors.** (Hint: There are two.)

1. _____

How would you evaluate this behavior?

1	2	3	4	5	6	7	8	9	10
Not Smart			**Fairly Smart**				**Very Smart**		

2. _____

How would you evaluate this behavior?

1	2	3	4	5	6	7	8	9	10
Not Smart			**Fairly Smart**				**Very Smart**		

Now write down each of Rebecca's **attitudes.** (Hint: There are two.)

1. _____

How would you evaluate this attitude?

1	2	3	4	5	6	7	8	9	10
Not Smart			**Fairly Smart**				**Very Smart**		

2. _____

How would you evaluate this attitude?

1	2	3	4	5	6	7	8	9	10
Not Smart			**Fairly Smart**				**Very Smart**		

Predict the consequences of Rebecca's attitudes and behavior.

Her grades:_____

Possible   Probable

Her relationship with her parents: _____

Possible   Probable

Her chances of getting into a good college: _____

Possible   Probable

Follow the same procedure with Matthew's behaviors and attitudes about recording assignments. Underline each behavior once and double underline each attitude. (Hint: You should be able to find at least three behaviors and six attitudes.)

Write down each of Matthew's **behaviors.**

1. _____

How would you evaluate this behavior?

1	2	3	4	5	6	7	8	9	10
Not Smart			**Fairly Smart**				**Very Smart**		

2. _____

How would you evaluate this behavior?

1	2	3	4	5	6	7	8	9	10
Not Smart			**Fairly Smart**				**Very Smart**		

3. _____

How would you evaluate this behavior?

1	2	3	4	5	6	7	8	9	10
Not Smart			**Fairly Smart**				**Very Smart**		

Now write down each of Matthew's **attitudes.**

1. _____

How would you evaluate this attitude?

1	2	3	4	5	6	7	8	9	10
Not Smart			**Fairly Smart**				**Very Smart**		

2. _____

How would you evaluate this attitude?

1	2	3	4	5	6	7	8	9	10
Not Smart			**Fairly Smart**				**Very Smart**		

3. _____

How would you evaluate this attitude?

1	2	3	4	5	6	7	8	9	10
Not Smart			**Fairly Smart**				**Very Smart**		

4. _____

How would you evaluate this attitude?

1	2	3	4	5	6	7	8	9	10
Not Smart			**Fairly Smart**				**Very Smart**		

5. _____

How would you evaluate this attitude?

1	2	3	4	5	6	7	8	9	10
Not Smart			**Fairly Smart**				**Very Smart**		

6. _____

How would you evaluate this attitude?

1	2	3	4	5	6	7	8	9	10
Not Smart			**Fairly Smart**				**Very Smart**		

Predict the consequences of Matthew's attitudes and behavior.

His grades:_____

                          Possible Probable

His relationship with his parents: _____

                          Possible Probable

His relationship with his teachers: _____

                          Possible Probable

His chances of getting into a college: _____

                          Possible Probable

His chances of getting into a vocational training program: _____

                          Possible Probable

A SYSTEM FOR RECORDING ASSIGNMENTS

Look at the following sample homework assignments. Assume today is Monday and that your teachers have written these assignments on the chalkboard in each of your classes.

Math: Due Tues.
p. 93 prob. 1–10
p. 96 prob. 1–8
show work (not just answers)

French: Begin studying past perfect tense p. 26
Quiz Wed. all vrbs p. 26–34

Government: Due Tues.
rd. pp. 156–165
ans. ques. 1–5 p. 166
complt. sen.—skip line betwn answ.
Chap. Test Fri.

Biology: Due Tues.
rd. pp. 87–109
Know defin. 10 words pg. 105
Paper due Mon. 2/10

English: Due Wed.
Analyze poem D. H. Lawrence p. 130
Book rpt. due 2/21

As you can see, certain assignments are due the following day, Tuesday. The French teacher has scheduled a quiz on Wednesday, and the Government teacher has scheduled a chapter test on Friday. A biology paper is due the following Monday. A book report is due in two weeks.

Of course, teachers don't always write assignments on the chalkboard. Some hand out a homework assignment sheet. (You'll examine methods for effectively using homework handouts later in this unit.) Other teachers announce homework assignments orally. Recording information when the assignments are announced orally can be more challenging because you must listen carefully and try to make sense out of the assignment while you're writing.

Look at the **Sample Assignment Sheet** that follows. Note that Monday's typical homework assignments in several subjects have been recorded on this sheet. The sample assignment sheet is designed to model an effective way to use an assignment sheet.

Recording an Assignment

For practice, transfer the assignment written above onto **Practice Assignment Sheet I** (page 72). For guidance, refer to the **Sample Assignment Sheet** on page 71 and use the method modeled in the sample to record the information. To make the information fit, use abbreviations such as "Tues." and "p" for page.

Common Abbreviations:

(If you wish, omit periods after abbreviations.)

Hint: leave out vowels whenever possible, but make certain you understand your abbreviations.

bg. = begin	M.T. = midterm	s.w. = show work
ch. = chapter	p. = page	T. = test
comp. = complete	prac. = practice	th.= the
corr. = correct	prob. = problem	t/o = throughout
d. = due	Q. = quiz	u. = unit
ex.= example	rvw. = review	v. = very
exer. = exercises	rd.= read	w/ = with
F. = final exam	rpt. = report	w/o = without
f.d. = final draft	sec. = section	
imp. = important	st. = study	

SAMPLE ASSIGNMENT SHEET

WEEK OF: <u>10/24/05</u>

SUBJECTS	MONDAY	TUESDAY	WEDNESDAY	THURSDAY	FRIDAY
MATH	P. 93 PROB. 1-10 P. 96 PROB. 1-8 S. W.				
FRENCH	PST PERFCT P. 26 Q. WED. P. 26–34				
GOV'T.	RD. P. 156–165 ANS. QUES. 1-5 P. 166 CMPLT SEN /SKP LNE CH TEST FRI 2/7				
BIOLOGY	RD. P. 87–109 KNOW DEF. 10 WRDS P. 105. RPT DUE MON. 2/10				
ENGLISH	ANLYZE POEM DH LAWRENCE P. 130 D. Wed. BK RPT D. 2/21				
TESTS & REPORTS	GVT. T. 2/7 BIO. RPT. 2/10 FR. QUIZ WED ENG. BK RPT D. 2/21				

PRACTICE ASSIGNMENT SHEET I					
WEEK OF:					
SUBJECTS	**MONDAY**	**TUESDAY**	**WEDNESDAY**	**THURSDAY**	**FRIDAY**
MATH					
FRENCH					
GOV'T.					
BIOLOGY					
ENGLISH					
TESTS & REPORTS					

Practice Writing Down Assignments

Record the following homework on the Practice Assignment Sheet II on page 74. Use the "Sample Assignment Sheet" as a model. Write legibly and use abbreviations to save time and space.

Math: Due Tues.
p. 17
prob. 1–8
show work

Physics: Due Tues.
pp. 81–84
p. 85 exer. 1–6
hand in lab book

Due Wed.
rd. pp. 18–26
p. 27 prob. 1–3
Due Thurs.
p. 28 prob. 1–3
show work
Due Fri.
p. 25 prob. 1–10
p. 29 probs. 1, 3, 5, 7

Due Wed.
p. 90 ques. 1–7

Due Thurs.
p. 91 exer. 1–9
workbook pp. 97–99
Due Fri.
exer. p. 99 1–8
Ch. 4 test

Spanish: Due Tues.
study voc. words p. 32
Due Wed.
voc. test ch. 4
Due Fri.
grammar rules
pp. 29–31

English: Due Tues.
pp. 51–54
Voc. p. 55
Due Wed.
pp. 59–60
p. 61 exer. 1–5
Due Thurs.
pp. 62–65
p. 66 exer. 1–6

Due Fri.
pp. 67–69
p. 70 exer. 1–6
Book Report

Social Studies: Due Tues.
Read pp. 34–45

Due Wed.
Read pp. 45–56
Quiz Unit 1 Friday
Due Thurs.
Ans Ques.
pp. 43–44 1–9
Due Fri.
Quiz

Using Your Assignment Sheet

You may already have your own effective method for recording assignments, and you may have used this method for several years. Perhaps you purchased an assignment book in a store, or you've gotten in the habit of writing down homework on a piece of binder paper. Although you may be happy with your present method, you may discover that the **Study Max** method actually works better.

As an experiment, use the **Study Max** assignment sheets for the next two weeks. If you're not pleased with the system, modify it or find another method that you like better. What's important is to use an assignment recording sheet every day so that you don't forget to do your homework, hand in your assignments on time, or follow your teachers' instructions.

PRACTICE ASSIGNMENT SHEET II					
WEEK OF:					
SUBJECTS	**MONDAY**	**TUESDAY**	**WEDNESDAY**	**THURSDAY**	**FRIDAY**
MATH					
PHYSICS					
SPANISH					
ENGLISH					
SOCIAL STUDIES					
TESTS & REPORTS					

USING TEACHER-PREPARED ASSIGNMENT HANDOUTS

If your teachers provide weekly homework assignment handouts, knowing precisely what you need to do is obviously simplified. To use these handouts properly, you must

- Carefully read the handout for each subject.
- Make certain that you complete everything that's been assigned.
- Follow the directions precisely.
- Submit your work when it's due.

SUBJECTS	MONDAY	TUESDAY	WEDNESDAY	THURSDAY	FRIDAY
_____					
_____					
_____					
_____					
_____					
TESTS & REPORTS					

STUDY MAX ASSIGNMENT SHEET

WEEK OF:

- Allocate time for long-range obligations such as studying for tests and writing reports.

It's recommended that you use highlight pens in different colors to identify the key information on homework handouts. (It is also recommended that you use the following highlighting method when you record your assignments on the Study Max form.)

- Use one color to indicate specific problems or exercises that must be completed.
- Use a second color to indicate specific details or instructions.
- Use a third color to indicate when each assignment is due.

Make up a code that indicates what each color represents and consistently use these specific colors with all teacher homework handouts. For example, you might always use yellow to indicate the specific problems or exercises that need to be completed. After each assignment is completed, put a check mark above it. This procedure will ensure that you cover all the bases when you do your homework.

For practice, use the highlighting procedures described here with the following sample history assignment. If you don't have highlighters with you, complete this exercise at home.

History Assignment

Read Unit 3, pages 64–85 Answer questions on page 86. Do even-numbered questions (#'s 2, 4, 6, and 8). Complete sentences. Skip line between each answer. Write your name next to the red margin on the top line and write the date below it. Due tomorrow.

To make sure that you don't lose your homework handouts, insert them in a labeled plastic sleeve or folder in your binder. Your teacher may have done most of the work for you, but you must still make certain that you're properly using the homework handout.

LAUNCHING YOUR HOMEWORK-RECORDING SYSTEM

Unless you already have an effective, tried-and-true assignment-recording system or your teachers provide weekly homework handouts, you should begin using the Study Max Assignment Sheet today. Even if you've already written down your assignments using your old method, it's recommended that you transfer the information to the Study Max Assignment Sheet so that you can evaluate each method and decide which one you like best. Make sure to write down *all* the important details. Forgetting to record that a history test is scheduled for next Friday could be a disaster!

Having an assignment sheet will help you become better organized. You'll know what your specific homework responsibilities are each evening, and you'll have the precise instructions handy. The sheets have space for one week's assignments, and you can make as many copies as you need. Label a section in your binder "Assignments." Punch holes in the assignment sheets and put them in this section.

At first, using assignment sheets may seem like extra work. After a while, it will become a habit, and you'll automatically use the system without even thinking about it.

Unit 4

Organizing Study Materials

For Teachers

Objectives

This unit presents practical organization techniques that are designed to help students study and do homework more efficiently.

LESSON PLAN

1. Students read the introductory case study, **Organizing and Tackling Homework** and list each of Megan's homework-related attitudes and behaviors. They evaluate these behaviors and predict the possible or probable consequences.
2. Students list the materials they need to do their homework and practice using three organizational checklists during a one-week experiment.
3. Students organize their binders by labeling their subjects. They create a specific section for their study schedule, assignment sheets, and organizational checklists.

THE NEED FOR ORGANIZATION

Good study skills and good organizational skills are intrinsically linked. Successful students plan ahead, record their assignments accurately, and make certain they have essential study materials. At the end of the day, they verify that they've put their assignment sheet, textbooks, handouts, graded tests, corrected homework, and binders into their backpacks. When they sit down after school to study, they make sure they have the pens, paper, ruler, and dictionary they require to complete their homework.

Disorganized students are at the opposite end of the efficiency spectrum. They frequently forget to bring home from school the essential materials they need to do their homework. Their desks are usually a mess, their rooms are disaster areas, and their notebooks are in disarray. If they actually bother to write down their assignments, they often record incomplete and inaccurate information (see Unit 3). The academic consequences are predictable. Chronically disorganized students typically

- Spend more time looking for things than actually working.
- Study inefficiently.
- Produce substandard work.
- Generate stress for everyone affected by their maladaptive behavior.

Lecturing disorganized students is generally a waste of time. Those with the greatest need to alter their maladaptive behavior are usually the most resistant to change. Associating advice and recommendations with nagging, they tune out the lectures and insist on doing things their way.

Chronic patterns of disorganization established in childhood could persist throughout life. If students are to break these counterproductive habits, they must be

- Provided with practical guidelines for effective organization.
- Taught how to use their study materials more efficiently.
- Furnished with opportunities to practice and assimilate organization procedures.

Students who waste their study time searching for their textbooks, handouts, binders, homework assignments, paper, pencils, dictionaries, pens, calculators, and lecture notes must be guided to a key realization: Improved organization can make their schoolwork easier and their efforts more productive. The starting point is to furnish students with methodical procedures for making certain they have the materials they need to do their homework and study productively and to provide them with an easy-to-learn and easy-to-apply template that incorporates practical hands-on techniques for organizing their binder and study area.

As students assimilate basic organizational principles and practices and begin to derive the benefits of improved organization (i.e., reduced stress and improved grades), their resistance to creating order in their lives should begin to shift. The goal is for them to willingly incorporate sound organizational procedures into their daily academic modus operandi.

SUMMARY OF STUDENT
EXERCISES AND ACTIVITIES

Examining the Story

Students read an anecdote that describes a student with good study behaviors and a student with poor study behaviors. They identify and evaluate each of Megan's productive behaviors and attitudes and predict their consequences. They then identify and evaluate each of her counterproductive behaviors and attitudes and predict their consequences.

Students examine three basic organizational checklists. These checklists indicate the essential materials they need to bring home from school, take to school, and have available when studying. Encourage students to try a one-week experiment in which they use the checklists everyday and keep track of their performance (i.e., grades on homework assignments and tests). At the end of the experiment, students should discuss their reactions to the organizational system and its effect on their performance. Be prepared for resistance from some students to the idea of using checklists because such a system requires applied self-discipline, a quality that many academically underperforming students clearly lack. Emphasize that the checking-off procedure will quickly become a habit that they will be able to perform mentally. Once they've assimilated the organizational procedures, using "formal" checklists will be optional. (Students who are having difficulty assimilating efficient organizational behaviors should be encouraged to continue using the checklist system for a more protracted period.)

A System for Getting Organized and Organizing Your Binder

Students learn a step-by-step procedure for organizing their binders. Chronically disorganized students will probably require extra monitoring to make certain they're following the steps and using the system consistently. You can certainly hand off this responsibility to their parents. A photocopied letter home, a telephone call, or a mini parent conference in which you define the problem and explain the strategy for correcting the problem should do the trick.

Unit 4

Organizing Study Materials

For Students

ORGANIZING AND TACKLING HOMEWORK

Megan returned home from volleyball practice at 5:30. After gulping down a glass of milk, she headed to her room. She wanted to use the thirty minutes before dinner to get some of her homework done. She sat down at her desk, turned on her desk lamp, and pulled her math textbook from her backpack. She could always tell which one it was without even having to look. It was the biggest and heaviest one in the pack.

Taking out her binder, Megan turned to her weekly assignment sheet and quickly scanned it to determine how much studying she had to do that evening. She noted when the next quizzes and tests were scheduled and confirmed when her English book report was due. She then glanced at the study schedule she had taped on the wall in front of her desk. Although she had quite a bit of homework, she was confident that she could complete it in the two hours and forty-five minutes that she had budgeted. Even with some study breaks, she would still have more than an hour to watch TV and talk with her friends on the phone before she went to bed.

Megan's math assignment was to do all the problems on pages 79 and 83. On her assignment sheet, she had written, "p. 79 & 83 all prob./show wrk." She reached for some loose-leaf paper on the shelf above her desk, took a pencil from the desk drawer, and began to work. It took twenty-five minutes to complete the assignment. She finished with about two minutes to spare before her mom called her to come down for dinner.

When she returned to her desk after dinner, Megan looked at her English assignment. She had written on her assignment sheet, "Analyze poem T. S. Elliot. Discuss rhyme, meter, and imagery. Min. 2 pgs. Due Wed. Follow stand. format." She took out the mimeographed copy of the poem her teacher had handed out and began to read it carefully. She made notes in the margin about the meter, which was iambic pentameter, and she began to analyze the content and imagery in the poem. Once she finished taking notes, she began to write a first draft of her essay. She planned to revise, edit, proofread, and recopy her paper the following evening.

When Megan looked at the clock, she discovered that she had worked for fifty-five minutes on her essay. She put her notes and first-draft into the section in her binder labeled "English," and she took a ten-minute break to call Rebecca. Returning to her desk, she checked her assignment sheet again and began her history homework. She read the assigned pages, took notes, and answered the six questions at the end of the unit. The assignment required approximately forty minutes. Megan decided to take a ten-minute break and went to the kitchen for a snack.

Once she was back in her room, Megan again looked at her assignment sheet to find out what her Spanish homework was. She turned to Chapter 7 and began to study the dialogue and pronounce the new vocabulary words. She confirmed some of the definitions by looking up the words in her Spanish dictionary. She took out a box of colored felt markers and began to write down the assigned words on index cards. She chose a different felt pen for each word and wrote each definition in a different color on the back of the index card. Closing her eyes, Megan tried to see each word and its definition in the color she had chosen in her "mind's eye." Her teacher had taught the class this memory trick, and Megan found that it helped her remember the spelling and definitions of the words. (The technique of visualizing information in your mind is examined in Unit 9.) Her Spanish assignment required thirty-five minutes.

When she looked at her assignment sheet again, Megan was delighted to discover that her biology teacher hadn't assigned much homework. She quickly scanned the ten pages and then read the material again more slowly. She planned to take notes on the assigned pages the following evening. Her entire biology assignment required only twenty-five minutes. Mrs. Washington must have been in a good mood, Megan concluded.

Her homework was finished. Megan had studied for approximately two hours and forty-five minutes, if she included the two study breaks she had taken. This was what she had budgeted. She put her books, papers, and binder in her backpack. The first thing she had to do now was call Todd. They had to decide whether they were going to the concert or to Nicole's party on Saturday night.

EXAMINING THE STORY

The description of Megan's study procedure gives you clues about what kind of student she is and describes her study strategy. Go back into the story and see how many of Megan's specific actions (or procedures) you can identify. Underline each action and number it in the order in which it occurred. Believe it or not, approximately *thirty-eight specific actions were described.* You may find fewer because you may be combining two separate actions that are found in the same sentence. If you can find twenty-five or more specific actions, you've done well. Use a pencil because you may want to erase and change your numbering as you go along.

Evaluating Megan's Study System

Evaluate Megan's procedure of doing her homework at a desk.

1	2	3	4	5	6	7	8	9	10
Not Smart			**Fairly Smart**				**Very Smart**		

Evaluate Megan's procedure of making sure she has the supplies she needs to do her homework.

1	2	3	4	5	6	7	8	9	10
Not Smart			**Fairly Smart**				**Very Smart**		

Evaluate Megan's procedure of taping her schedule on the wall in front of her desk.

1	2	3	4	5	6	7	8	9	10
Not Smart			**Fairly Smart**				**Very Smart**		

Evaluate Megan's decision to use an assignment sheet.

1	2	3	4	5	6	7	8	9	10
Not Smart			**Fairly Smart**				**Very Smart**		

How would you evaluate Megan's overall study procedure?

1	2	3	4	5	6	7	8	9	10
Not Smart			**Fairly Smart**				**Very Smart**		

Predicting What Is Likely to Happen

After examining Megan's study methods, you should be able to make some predictions about the consequences of her procedure. Indicate whether the consequence is possible or probable.

Her grades in school: _____

Possible   Probable

Her parents' attitude about her effort and conscientiousness: _____

Possible   Probable

Her teacher's attitude about her effort and conscientiousness: _____

Possible   Probable

Her chances of getting into college: _____

Possible   Probable

A SYSTEM FOR GETTING ORGANIZED

You may be thinking, "I'm not sure I ever want to be as organized as Megan! It seems like it would be too much work."

In the long run, being organized actually requires *less* work! Once you've created an effective organizational system, you will spend less time looking for what you need. You'll be able to study more efficiently, and your homework will be easier to manage and complete. The time you used to spend "spinning your wheels" can now be spent doing things you really enjoy.

Having the Necessary Materials

Have you ever sat down to do a homework assignment and discovered that you had left your textbook or an important handout at school? Have you ever realized that you didn't have binder paper, a pen, or a dictionary to look up your assigned vocabulary words? The following three checklists can make your life more organized.

CHECKLIST 1: Materials and supplies you need to bring home each day from school.

CHECKLIST 2: Materials and supplies you need to have when you leave for school in the morning.

CHECKLIST 3: Materials you need in your study area at home to do your homework.

These checklists don't have to be complicated. For example:

CHECKLIST 1. MATERIALS TO BRING HOME FROM SCHOOL

	Mon.	Tues.	Wed.	Thurs.	Fri.
Binder	_____	_____	_____	_____	_____
Textbooks	_____	_____	_____	_____	_____
Assignment Sheet	_____	_____	_____	_____	_____
Workbooks	_____	_____	_____	_____	_____
Assigned Homework	_____	_____	_____	_____	_____
Handouts	_____	_____	_____	_____	_____
Corrected Assignments	_____	_____	_____	_____	_____
Graded Tests	_____	_____	_____	_____	_____
_____	_____	_____	_____	_____	_____
_____	_____	_____	_____	_____	_____
_____	_____	_____	_____	_____	_____
_____	_____	_____	_____	_____	_____

List other materials or supplies you might need (ruler, protractor, compass, Spanish or French dictionary, highlighting pen, etc.) in the blank spaces at the end of the checklist. Because Checklist 1 is so simple, you should be able to complete it in your head after using it for a few days. The checklist will become an automatic habit. Checklists 2 and 3 are also simple to use.

CHECKLIST 2. MATERIALS TO BRING TO SCHOOL FROM HOME

	Mon.	Tues.	Wed.	Thurs.	Fri.
Binder	_____	_____	_____	_____	_____
Textbooks	_____	_____	_____	_____	_____
Assignment Sheet	_____	_____	_____	_____	_____
Workbooks	_____	_____	_____	_____	_____
Completed Homework	_____	_____	_____	_____	_____
Paper	_____	_____	_____	_____	_____
Pencils	_____	_____	_____	_____	_____

Graded Tests and Assignments	_____	_____	_____	_____	_____
_____	_____	_____	_____	_____	_____
_____	_____	_____	_____	_____	_____
_____	_____	_____	_____	_____	_____
_____	_____	_____	_____	_____	_____

CHECKLIST 3. STUDY ENVIRONMENT AT HOME

	Mon.	Tues.	Wed.	Thurs.	Fri.
Few Distractions	_____	_____	_____	_____	_____
Quiet Study Area	_____	_____	_____	_____	_____
Work at Desk or Table	_____	_____	_____	_____	_____
Labeled Folders for Completed Work Being Left at Home	_____	_____	_____	_____	_____
Folders Filed Alphabetically in a Drawer	_____	_____	_____	_____	_____
Dictionaries	_____	_____	_____	_____	_____
Paper	_____	_____	_____	_____	_____
Ruler	_____	_____	_____	_____	_____
Pencils and Pens	_____	_____	_____	_____	_____
Good Lighting	_____	_____	_____	_____	_____
_____	_____	_____	_____	_____	_____
_____	_____	_____	_____	_____	_____
_____	_____	_____	_____	_____	_____
_____	_____	_____	_____	_____	_____

As you can see, these checklists require only a few seconds to complete. If you use them consistently for a few days, the procedure will become a habit.

Try an experiment for the next week. Check off the items on the list every day. If you find that you're spending less time looking for things, continue using the checklist. Before long, you'll no longer need to use a formal checklist. You'll probably be able to keep track of the materials you need and monitor the study conditions mentally.

ORGANIZING YOUR BINDER

You may already have a system for organizing your binder, and you may be convinced you can find everything you need to do your work. Look at the following suggested steps and decide whether your system is as efficient as it could be. If your binder is a mess, consider following these steps carefully:

_____ **STEP 1.** Buy dividers for each subject.

_____ **STEP 2.** Label a specific section in the front of your binder **Assignment Recording Sheets**.

_____ **STEP 3.** Label a specific section in your binder **Study Schedule.** (Tape or tack a second copy of this schedule to the wall or desk in your study area at home.) Buy a plastic sleeve or cover and place your schedule inside it so it doesn't get torn or dirty. Place the plastic sleeve containing your **Study Schedule** in your binder after the **Assignment Sheet** section. (You could also tape your study schedule to the front inside cover of your binder.)

_____ **STEP 4.** On the divider tabs, list each of your subjects: (**Math, History, Science, Study Skills, etc.**).

_____ **STEP 5.** If you want to keep some papers in your binder and they don't have holes, use a hole puncher.

_____ **STEP 6.** Buy reinforcements and put them over the holes so your papers won't fall out of your binder.

_____ **STEP 7.** Put all important papers, returned homework, and returned tests in your binder. Make sure to put a date on these papers.

If you always know where to find the study materials you need, you'll spend less time searching for them. You can spend this time getting your work done. Then you'll have more free time. *Organization makes life easier, not harder!*

Take a minute to answer the following questions. They should crystallize your own thinking and attitudes about organization.

True-False Statements About Organization

Only morons use checklists.	**True**	**False**
Forgetting a textbook you need to do your homework is exciting.	**True**	**False**
If you're getting good grades, don't worry about being organized.	**True**	**False**
Completing material and supply checklists requires at least an extra fifteen minutes every day.	**True**	**False**

It's OK to miss deadlines and forget assignments.	**True**	**False**
Organized people are robots.	**True**	**False**
Organization destroys creativity.	**True**	**False**
Losing your assignments and having to search for them adds excitement to your life.	**True**	**False**
Having a room that's a disaster area is guaranteed to make life with your parents a pleasure.	**True**	**False**
Organization requires more time in the long run.	**True**	**False**
You can be efficient and not be well organized.	**True**	**False**
Once using a supply checklist becomes habit, you can run through the list mentally.	**True**	**False**
Your binder is for carrying papers. You don't need to organize it. Just jam your stuff in it.	**True**	**False**
You don't have to worry about being organized until you go to college or get a job.	**True**	**False**
Organization causes people to become brain dead.	**True**	**False**
Searching for the things you need can be great fun.	**True**	**False**
If you're bright, you don't need to be organized.	**True**	**False**

Unit 5

Creating a Smart Study Environment

For Teachers

Objectives

This unit shows students how to create a study environment at home that is conducive to productive learning.

LESSON PLAN

1. In **Operating at Peak Performance,** students critically evaluate another student's counterproductive study procedure and predict the potential consequences of his attitudes and behaviors. They examine the issue of distractions while studying, take a look at rationalizations for studying ineffectually, and explore ideas for improving their study environment.

2. In **Chaos: Doing Too Many Things at Once,** students examine specific situations that underscore the disadvantages of trying to function in a distracting environment and make predictions about the consequences of these behaviors. They then evaluate productive and counterproductive study environments.

3. In **A Sheltered Study Island**, students list and evaluate the specific positive features that are characteristic of a nondistracting study environment.

Students then describe the specific features of a distracting study environment and make predictions about the consequences of studying in such an environment.

4. Students explore specific ways to improve their at-home study environment. They do an experiment that reinforces the organizational concepts taught in the unit and measure the effects of studying in a nondistracting context.

CONTROLLING THE STUDY ENVIRONMENT

Many high school students study and learn inefficiently because they insist on doing their homework while watching TV or listening to loud music. These same students also typically interrupt their studying with repeated phone calls, trips to the kitchen, video games, and Internet surfing.

Ironically, students with the greatest need to concentrate when studying are often the ones who surround themselves with the most distractions. These teenagers argue that they can study *better* with the TV or stereo playing. Some professionals actually support this position. Describing modern students as "iPod Learners," they maintain that many teenagers can actually study productively under less-than-ideal conditions because they've been exposed repeatedly to intrusive "background noise" since early childhood. Whereas many adults would struggle to concentrate in a distracting environment, these educators contend that children have become habituated and inured to the sounds of the TV, video games, and loud pulsating music, and they also contend that insisting students turn off the TV or stereo when doing homework will not necessarily improve their academic performance. This position is certainly not universally shared, however. Many teachers and learning specialists are convinced by their own extensive frontline experiences that students who study in a noisy environment often learn ineffectually and that those with attention-deficit/hyperactivity disorder (ADHD) are especially vulnerable to distracting auditory and visual stimuli. (See *Roadblocks to Learning* [Greene, 2002] for a more comprehensive examination of ADHD.)

This unit supports the position of educators who are convinced of the benefits of a nondistracting learning context. The exercises and activities are designed to teach students how to enhance their school performance by intentionally regulating their at-home study environment and by intentionally eliminating or reducing the factors that could interfere with their learning efficiency and focus. Although deliberate "environmental control" will not necessarily resolve the chronic concentration problems typically associated with ADHD, it can be of great value to students who are learning inefficiently because they haven't figured out the logical "do's and don'ts" of productive studying. Even students who are doing acceptable work may benefit from making judicious modifications in their study environment. By reducing distractions and focusing more intently, they may discover that they can significantly improve their grades.

Lecturing about the need for good study habits and a quiet study environment is likely to trigger defensiveness and resistance. The far more effective strategy is to guide students to a key realization: They can improve their grades and reduce their study time by reducing background noise when they do their homework.

SUMMARY OF STUDENT EXERCISES AND ACTIVITIES

Examining the Story

Students read the introductory anecdote, identify and evaluate Jamal's counterproductive study procedures, and predict the effects of his behavior on his grades and his relationship with his parents. They examine arguments that Jamal might offer to justify his study methods. They then speculate what Megan (the highly organized student described in the case study in Unit 4) might hypothetically suggest to help Jamal improve his study habits.

The activity asks students to create a hypothetical dialogue presenting both sides of the "distractions versus no distractions" controversy. By having your students analyze and critique another student's study habits, you're less likely to trigger defensiveness and resistance.

During a class discussion, students brainstorm how Jamal might improve his grades. They apply what they've already learned about strategic thinking and studying and practice key cause-and-effect principles that run thematically through the **Study Max Program.** The goal is to guide students to the realization that their insights about improving Jamal's school performance can and should be integrated into their own study procedures.

Chaos: Doing Too Many Things at Once

This exercise examines the inherent challenges in trying to concentrate on more than one thing at a time. Students evaluate different hypothetical study situations and identify the cause-and-effect link between effective studying and good grades.

A Sheltered Study Island

This activity encourages students to visualize their study context as a quiet, nondistracting, environmentally controlled "study island." Students describe ideal study conditions, and they list and evaluate specific features that are conducive to effectual studying. They then discuss the specific features of a disorganized environment that is not conducive to effective studying and predict the effects of doing their homework in this context. These activities unequivocally underscore the logical benefits of deliberately controlling the environment when studying.

Reducing Distractions

These exercises ask students to apply the organizational principles they've examined and to make a list of concrete steps they could take to improve their own study environment. They apply these guidelines during a two-week experiment and monitor their subsequent grades on homework assignments and tests. If students are able to see demonstrable improvement in their performance, they're more likely to be receptive to integrating commonsense distraction-reducing procedures into their own daily study modus operandi.

Unit 5

Creating a Smart Study Environment

For Students

OPERATING AT PEAK PERFORMANCE

It was 5:30 p.m., and Jamal was lying on his stomach facing the end of his bed. His head was propped in his hands, and his Spanish textbook and binder were lying on the bed in front of him. After quickly glancing through the unit, Jamal reached for his binder and began to write down the irregular -ir conjugations that his teacher had assigned. Jamal knew there would be a quiz on these verbs the next day, and he had to get at least a C if he was going to keep his grade above D.

Every few seconds, Jamal would glance at the TV to find out what was happening on his favorite sitcom. From time to time, his eyes would wander back to his textbook, and he would write down another conjugation. When the commercials came on, Jamal finished writing the conjugations, and he started to write down the new vocabulary words he had to learn. He hoped he could finish his Spanish assignment before Monday Night Football started. He never missed Monday Night Football, and tonight his favorite team, the New York Jets, was playing the San Francisco 49ers. Jamal was certain that the Jets would win. He planned to do his science homework during halftime. His math homework would have to wait until the end of the game, assuming the game didn't go into overtime. If it did, he would have to do his math homework on the bus in the morning.

Jamal often finished his math homework on the school bus, and he was convinced that this was "no big deal." Working on the bus, however, was particularly difficult on Tuesday mornings because all of his friends would want to talk about the football game. Jamal would invariably join this discussion, and unfortunately this often resulted in an incomplete math assignment with lots of careless mistakes.

EXAMINING THE STORY

In this story, a series of specific study behaviors are described. Underline and number in order each of these behaviors. Then summarize each behavior in the following list. See if you can find nine.

Behavior 1:   Jamal studied lying on his bed.

Behavior 2:   _____

Behavior 3:   _____

Behavior 4:   _____

Behavior 5:   _____

Behavior 6:   _____

Behavior 7:   _____

Behavior 8:   _____

Behavior 9:   _____

How would you evaluate Jamal's decision to do his homework while lying on his bed?

1	2	3	4	5	6	7	8	9	10
Not Smart			**Fairly Smart**				**Very Smart**		

What are the possible consequences of this decision? _____

How would you evaluate Jamal's decision to do his homework while watching TV?

1	2	3	4	5	6	7	8	9	10
Not Smart			**Fairly Smart**				**Very Smart**		

Predicting What Is Likely to Happen

Assume Jamal studies this way for all of his courses. Predict the consequences.

His parents' reaction to his study procedures: _____

Possible   Probable

Why did you make this prediction? _____

_____

His grades in school: _____

Possible   Probable

Why did you make this prediction? _____

_____

Examining the Other Side

Write down the arguments that you would expect Jamal to use to justify his study procedures.

1. _____

2. _____

3. _____

Describe an argument that Jamal might have with his parents about his study habits. What would his parents probably say? _____

_____

What would Jamal probably say? _____

_____

Why would his parents be concerned? _____

_____

How would you evaluate his parents' concern?

1	2	3	4	5	6	7	8	9	10
Unreasonable			**Reasonable**				**Very Reasonable**		

Quickly reread the case study about Megan at the beginning of Unit 4. Imagine that Megan is one of Jamal's friends and that Jamal decides he wants to improve his grades. Knowing that Megan is a good student, he asks her for advice. List some specific recommendations that you think she would make to help Jamal improve his schoolwork.

1. _____

2. _____

3. _____

4. _____

CHAOS: DOING TOO MANY THINGS AT ONCE

What do you think would happen if . . . ?

You take a test while thinking about the big argument you had with your best friend.

Consequence: _____

Possible   Probable

You try to study when you're very hungry.

Consequence: _____

Possible   Probable

You try to catch a pass while glancing at your girlfriend on the sidelines.

Consequence: _____

Possible   Probable

You try to listen to three conversations at once.

Consequence: _____

Possible   Probable

You try to explain to a friend how to solve a complicated algebra problem while watching an exciting scene in a movie.

Consequence: _____

Possible   Probable

You try to write an English essay while hanging out with your friends at the mall.

Consequence: _____

Possible   Probable

You try to study your science notes while riding on a skateboard.

Consequence: _____

Possible   Probable

Your dentist begins to work on your teeth while having an argument with his wife on a cell phone.

Consequence: _____

Possible   Probable

You study for a test when you're very sleepy.

Consequence: _____

Possible   Probable

Do you believe that you can do more than one thing at a time? Perhaps you're thinking, "Well, in some situations, I can do more than one thing at a time." It's true that sometimes you can work on several projects at once. For example, you could listen to the radio while driving, but you certainly couldn't drive safely while watching a portable TV. You could talk to a friend while playing catch, but you wouldn't want to have a conversation with someone while actually playing in a game. If you were the shortstop and you were talking with the third baseman when the ball is hit to you, you would probably make a fielding error because you weren't concentrating on the game. You can be certain that your coach would go *ballistic*. If you're at bat and you're thinking about what you're going to do on Saturday night, you're probably going to strike out.

In some respects, studying is like playing baseball. Your effort, attitude, and ability to concentrate will determine the quality of your game on the field and the quality of your grades on your report card. To do well, you must be motivated, give it your best shot, concentrate, and get the job done. This is the essence of operating at peak performance.

Evaluate the following situations:

Studying for a test while watching a basketball game on TV.

1	2	3	4	5	6	7	8	9	10
Not Smart			**Fairly Smart**				**Very Smart**		

Doing your history homework while sitting at a desk in your room.

1	2	3	4	5	6	7	8	9	10
Not Smart			**Fairly Smart**				**Very Smart**		

Talking on the telephone while writing a term paper.

1	2	3	4	5	6	7	8	9	10
Not Smart			**Fairly Smart**				**Very Smart**		

Closing the door to your room and studying hard for twenty-five minutes without a break.

1	2	3	4	5	6	7	8	9	10
Not Smart			**Fairly Smart**				**Very Smart**		

Repeatedly interrupting studying for a test to play video games with your brother.

1	2	3	4	5	6	7	8	9	10
Not Smart			**Fairly Smart**				**Very Smart**		

Copying your book report on the school bus.

1	2	3	4	5	6	7	8	9	10
Not Smart			**Fairly Smart**				**Very Smart**		

Doing your math problems while eating breakfast with your family.

1	2	3	4	5	6	7	8	9	10
Not Smart			**Fairly Smart**				**Very Smart**		

A SHELTERED STUDY ISLAND

There's a "trick" you can use to make your studying and homework easier and more productive. As you sit at your desk or table, pretend that you're on a peaceful, private island that has everything you need to do a first-rate job of studying: good light, supplies, assignment sheet, necessary textbooks, binder, and study schedule. Imagine that your island is quiet and organized, and you have intentionally eliminated distractions so that you can concentrate and work efficiently. Once you finish studying or are ready for a well-deserved study break, you can close your books, leave your study island, and "return to civilization."

In the spaces provided, list the specific features of an environmentally controlled "study island" that could improve your learning efficiency (for example, *no clutter*).

Detail 1: _____

Evaluate this feature (specifically, its effect on study efficiency).

1	2	3	4	5	6	7	8	9	10
Not Smart			**Fairly Smart**				**Very Smart**		

Detail 2: _____

Evaluate this feature.

1	2	3	4	5	6	7	8	9	10
Not Smart			**Fairly Smart**				**Very Smart**		

Detail 3: _____

Evaluate this feature.

1	2	3	4	5	6	7	8	9	10
Not Smart			**Fairly Smart**				**Very Smart**		

Detail 4: _____

Evaluate this feature.

1	2	3	4	5	6	7	8	9	10
Not Smart			**Fairly Smart**				**Very Smart**		

How difficult would it be for you to create a similar study island?

Not Difficult   Fairly Difficult   Very Difficult

How likely are you to create a similar study island?

Not Likely   Fairly Likely   Very Likely

How much do you believe your grades would improve if you did create a similar study island?

Not Much   Somewhat   A Great Deal

Now identify four features of a distracting study environment, and indicate how these conditions could interfere with effective studying.

1. _____

2. _____

3. _____

4. _____

Predict the consequences of a student studying in this environment. Underline your prediction.

Quality of Work:	Excellent	Good	Average	Below Average
Concentration:	Excellent	Good	Average	Below Average
Grades:	Excellent	Good	Average	Below Average

Reducing Distractions

List specific steps you could take to reduce distractions and improve your own study environment. For example, your list might include

- No TV or radio while studying.
- Study at a desk.
- Study for a minimum of twenty-five minutes before taking a break.

Include these steps if you wish. You do not necessarily have to have nine steps.

Steps to Reduce Distractions and Improve My Study Efficiency

1. _____

2. _____

3. _____

4. _____

5. _____

6. _____

7. _____

8. _____

9. _____

Experimenting With Reducing Distractions

You've already done an experiment in Unit 2 in which you kept track of your grades after developing a study schedule. Perhaps you're still in the middle of this experiment.

Stop the experiment even if you're still in the middle of it. Let's add another condition: studying with deliberately reduced distractions. During this new two-week experiment, maintain your study schedule and also follow the guidelines you created for reducing distractions. Record your grades on the form that follows. Make your best effort during the experiment. If your grades improve, you'll have *proven* that a study schedule and a good study environment can make a difference. It would obviously make sense to incorporate the procedures into your daily studying. They would provide you with a powerful "one-two punch."

**Tracking Your Grades
During the Combined Study Schedule
and Controlled Study Environment Experiment**

SUBJECT: _____

Homework:	Date ____ Grade ____	Date ____ Grade ____	Date ____ Grade ____
	Date ____ Grade ____	Date ____ Grade ____	Date ____ Grade ____
	Date ____ Grade ____	Date ____ Grade ____	Date ____ Grade ____
	Date ____ Grade ____	Date ____ Grade ____	Date ____ Grade ____
Tests:	Date ____ Grade ____	Date ____ Grade ____	Date ____ Grade ____
	Date ____ Grade ____	Date ____ Grade ____	Date ____ Grade ____
Reports/Papers:	Date ____ Grade ____	Date ____ Grade ____	Date ____ Grade ____
	Date ____ Grade ____	Date ____ Grade ____	Date ____ Grade ____

SUBJECT: _____

Homework:	Date ____ Grade ____	Date ____ Grade ____	Date ____ Grade ____
	Date ____ Grade ____	Date ____ Grade ____	Date ____ Grade ____
	Date ____ Grade ____	Date ____ Grade ____	Date ____ Grade ____
	Date ____ Grade ____	Date ____ Grade ____	Date ____ Grade ____

Tests: Date _____ Grade _____ Date _____ Grade _____ Date _____ Grade _____

Date _____ Grade _____ Date _____ Grade _____ Date _____ Grade _____

Reports/Papers: Date _____ Grade _____ Date _____ Grade _____ Date _____ Grade _____

Date _____ Grade _____ Date _____ Grade _____ Date _____ Grade _____

SUBJECT: _____

Homework: Date _____ Grade _____ Date _____ Grade _____ Date _____ Grade _____

Date _____ Grade _____ Date _____ Grade _____ Date _____ Grade _____

Date _____ Grade _____ Date _____ Grade _____ Date _____ Grade _____

Date _____ Grade _____ Date _____ Grade _____ Date _____ Grade _____

Tests: Date _____ Grade _____ Date _____ Grade _____ Date _____ Grade _____

Date _____ Grade _____ Date _____ Grade _____ Date _____ Grade _____

Reports/Papers: Date _____ Grade _____ Date _____ Grade _____ Date _____ Grade _____

Date _____ Grade _____ Date _____ Grade _____ Date _____ Grade _____

SUBJECT: _____

Homework: Date _____ Grade _____ Date _____ Grade _____ Date _____ Grade _____

Date _____ Grade _____ Date _____ Grade _____ Date _____ Grade _____

Date _____ Grade _____ Date _____ Grade _____ Date _____ Grade _____

Date _____ Grade _____ Date _____ Grade _____ Date _____ Grade _____

Tests: Date _____ Grade _____ Date _____ Grade _____ Date _____ Grade _____

Date _____ Grade _____ Date _____ Grade _____ Date _____ Grade _____

Reports/Papers: Date _____ Grade _____ Date _____ Grade _____ Date _____ Grade _____

Date _____ Grade _____ Date _____ Grade _____ Date _____ Grade _____

SUBJECT: _____

Homework: Date _____ Grade _____ Date _____ Grade _____ Date _____ Grade _____

Date _____ Grade _____ Date _____ Grade _____ Date _____ Grade _____

Date _____ Grade _____ Date _____ Grade _____ Date _____ Grade _____

Date _____ Grade _____ Date _____ Grade _____ Date _____ Grade _____

Tests: Date _____ Grade _____ Date _____ Grade _____ Date _____ Grade _____

Date _____ Grade _____ Date _____ Grade _____ Date _____ Grade _____

Reports/Papers: Date _____ Grade _____ Date _____ Grade _____ Date _____ Grade _____

Date _____ Grade _____ Date _____ Grade _____ Date _____ Grade _____

Don't allow yourself to become discouraged if your grades do not immediately improve. There's still a great deal to learn about how to study more productively.

In the next section of this book, you'll learn very powerful study methods that are designed to enhance your comprehension, recall, and test preparation skills. These methods, when combined with a controlled study environment, will help you to maximize your learning efficiency.

Part 3

Turbo Charging Reading and Studying

Unit 6

Power Reading

For Teachers

Objectives

This unit shows students how to use a pictorial method called "mind-mapping" or "chunking" to identify, record, and organize the information that they're studying. This technique of graphically representing data can be a potent resource for encouraging active learning, improving comprehension, and enhancing retention.

LESSON PLAN

1. In **Learning to Read With Muscle**, students are anecdotally introduced to the steps involved in the mind-mapping method. They use "question words" to convert the title of a facsimile history unit into a main idea question. They then record what they already know about the Hundred Years' War before reading the facsimile unit.

2. Students learn how to speed-read and use the method to scan the facsimile history unit. The objective is for them to use this tool to acquire a general overview of the content.

3. Students examine a sample mind-map of the first section of the Hundred Years' War unit. They discuss how the information is recorded and connected. They then carefully read the unit and mind-map the information. When they've finished, they examine and compare their mind-maps with a

completed modeled mind-map and note any important information they may have omitted.

4. Students review the **Six-Step Mind-Map Method**.

5. Using their mind-maps, students write a short essay to answer the title question that they posed in the first exercise.

6. As a homework or in-class assignment, students apply the mind-mapping method to an assignment in a content area textbook. They convert the title to a main idea question, speed-read, and mind-map.

BEYOND THE FUNDAMENTALS

One of the primary functions of grades K–3 in elementary school is to teach children the fundamentals of reading—namely, phonics, word attack, blending, tracking, and sight word recognition. This process of methodically developing students' basic ability to decode letters and words accurately is the first step in an extended instructional process that ideally leads to the acquisition of higher-level reading comprehension skills.

As children progress through elementary school, the focus of reading instruction shifts. Decoding is still emphasized, but students are also expected to understand and retain the content of what they read. In the upper grades of elementary school and in middle school, another shift in emphasis occurs. The basic retention of facts and literal information is no longer sufficient. Students are also expected to be able to utilize and apply the information they learn. This shift is reflected in textbooks that become increasingly cognitive in the upper grades.

Three different levels of reading comprehension can be delineated. On the **literal level**—the most basic—students are required to recall information. For example:

> **Literal Level:** The scientist placed the chemicals on the scale, weighed them carefully, placed the measured materials in a flask, and set the flask above the Bunsen burner.
>
> **Literal Question:** What were the steps of the scientist's procedure?

On the **inferential level** of comprehension, students must understand information that is implied, but not stated. For example:

> **Inferential Level:** The scientist placed the chemicals on the scale, weighed them carefully, placed the measured materials in a flask, and set the flask above the Bunsen burner.
>
> **Inferential Question:** What was the scientist doing?

On the **applicative level**—the highest level—students are required to utilize information. For example:

> **Applicative level:** The scientist placed the chemicals on the table, weighed them carefully, placed the measured materials in a flask, and set the flask above the Bunsen burner.

Applicative Question: What would you do if you were asked by your teacher to do a similar experiment?

Ideally, all students entering middle school should be able to comprehend and answer questions on all three levels of comprehension. The ongoing process of teaching students to utilize and critically evaluate the information that they read accelerates in high school. Those who can identify, understand, recall, draw inferences from, and apply information their teachers consider important are rewarded with good grades. The inclusive reading comprehension skills that students are expected to master are not only requisites to academic success in high school and college, they're also requisites to success in many of the more desirable vocations and careers.

The capacity to memorize facts and formulas (the literal level) certainly does not guarantee good grades in high school, particularly in advanced placement classes. Most teachers of college preparatory courses require that students be able to analyze what they're studying and apply what they're learning. They also expect students to have the thinking skills that allow them to ferret out underlying issues and implications and interpret information critically. Teachers in advanced courses, and especially instructors at the college level, require that their students also demonstrate that they are capable of understanding complex concepts and deriving *insight*, and they reward those who can think analytically and logically with superior grades.

That textbooks at the elementary and secondary level now incorporate material expressly designed to develop critical intelligence is unquestionably a positive trend. Some educators and publishers, however, believe that this trend is exceptionally innovative when, in point of fact, the systematic process of training students to think analytically and reason was first introduced more than 2,500 years ago by the Greek teacher-philosophers Socrates, Plato, and Aristotle. The current emphasis on critical thinking is considered groundbreaking only because so many U.S. schools over the last several decades have largely ignored critical intelligence and have focused primarily on the retention of facts, the mastery of basic skills, and the memorization of rules. Although the "new" critical thinking pedagogy may be little more than "reinventing the wheel," the effort in many schools to train students to progress beyond the simple regurgitation of facts and to think and read analytically is certainly laudable and long overdue.

Despite the current emphasis on teaching students to think critically, legions of American students are graduating each year from high school with glaringly deficient reading comprehension and analytical thinking skills. Most have the intellectual capacity to function on a higher intellectual level, but they often fail to do so because no one has systematically taught them how to analyze and "chew up" what they're reading. Habituated to mindless learning, these students haven't a clue about how to identify, classify, evaluate, link, assimilate, retain, and apply key information and concepts. After years of thinking and learning passively, they are for all intents and purposes cerebrally anesthetized. Studying translates into little more than a robotic process of turning the pages of their textbooks while they watch a favorite TV sitcom or listen to loud music.

To acquire advanced reading comprehension and analytical thinking skills, students must be taught how to

1. Identify important information.

2. Differentiate main ideas from details.

3. Understand underlying issues and concepts.

4. Critically evaluate content.

5. Retain facts.

6. Organize data.

7. Recognize the connections between what they're currently learning and what they've already learned.

8. Apply what they learn.

In the units that comprise Part 3: Turbo Charging Your Reading and Studying, students learn functional procedures that are easy to master and apply for attaining each of the objectives just enumerated. They'll also experiment with and practice using a range of comprehension-enhancing methodologies that incorporate different learning styles and preferences. The goal is for your students to select a particular learning strategy or to synthesize a combination of strategies that works for them and that enhances their learning efficiency and effectiveness.

MIND-MAPPING

Mind-mapping (also sometimes referred to as chunking) is a practical and engaging technique for organizing and representing information visually. This generally well-known method encourages students to think about how ideas and data are linked and helps them better understand, recall, and apply important information. Because most students find mind-mapping enjoyable, they tend to become more actively involved in the reading process when using the procedure. The net result is often improved comprehension and retention. Once students master the mind-mapping method, they can modify the procedure so that it conforms to their personal learning style and to the requirements of the particular courses they are taking. (In Unit 8, the more traditional note-taking method is introduced.)

SUMMARY OF STUDENT EXERCISES AND ACTIVITIES

Examining the Story

Students read an anecdote about a student who is intrigued by a powerful study method called mind-mapping that his older brother has taught him. They evaluate the protagonist's study attitudes and behavior, make predictions about the effects of his study procedures, and explain the rationale for their predictions. The goals are for your students to become equally intrigued by the mind-mapping method and for them to be motivated to learn and use this highly effective study tool.

Speed-Reading: Skimming for Information

Step 1 in learning how to mind-map is for students to turn the title of the unit into a main idea question. In Step 2, students are asked to consider what they already know about the subject. Most students probably know virtually nothing about the subject. Students then speed-read (or skim) the unit.

Emphasize that you do not expect students to remember all the details and that the goals of the skimming process are to acquire an overview of the content they are about to read and to enhance their awareness of how new information may be linked to what they already know.

When introducing speed-reading, you want to demonstrate how students should use their pointer and middle fingers as a horizontal "shutter" to facilitate skimming. (See the illustration on page 117 in the student section.) Instruct students to move their fingers quickly from left to right across each lines of text, and urge them to resist the temptation to subvocalize (pronounce the words their mind) when skimming. This is likely to prove challenging at first because students have been methodically trained in elementary school to read word by word. For most students, subvocalization is an entrenched habit, and they may be resistant to learning the new method. During the initial speed-reading process, emphasize that students should look simply for a "sense" of the key ideas. Most will need to practice the procedure several times before they begin to master the technique. Students will also require monitoring to ensure they're using the method properly.

Practicing Mind-Mapping

After speed-reading the unit, students read the material carefully and mind-map the content. A modeled mind-map of the introduction to the Hundred Years' War facsimile history unit is provided.

Once students have completed their mind-maps, they compare them with the model. They note and discuss any important information that they haven't included in their own mind-maps. To facilitate the discussion, you may want to copy the model on the chalkboard.

Students then reread the facsimile history unit, and at their desks they add additional information to their mind-maps. Another option would be to create a model mind-map on the chalkboard and to have your students tell you what important facts to add to the mind-map. These additions should be information they've included in their own maps. You (or the student offering the information) could insert the additions into the model. You can do a complete collective class mind-map or a partial class mind-map on two or three sections of the unit.

Once the class mind-map is complete (or a selected section has been mind-mapped), tell students to make certain they have included all the key information in their own mind-maps. If they wish, they can discard their original and create a new one. Urge them to be creative in their graphic designs and to use colored pencils or felt pens. For example, they might draw squiggly lines around each fact. Because creativity stimulates students to become involved actively and to visualize key information, it can significantly improve comprehension and retention.

Many students will complete their mind-map with little difficulty and will require minimal instruction. Others will need extra help and monitoring. If a significant number of students in your class have limited academic skills, it may be expedient to continue mind-mapping the entire unit on the chalkboard and, by so doing, demonstrate step-by-step how key information should be represented. You may want students to go to the chalkboard and map a section of the unit on the chalkboard while the rest of your students continue to work at their desks or in cooperative study groups. During a class discussion, you could examine why the student at the board has selected particular information to include or has chosen to represent the information in a particular way. Make the procedure enjoyable and stimulating, and use your judgment in expressing criticism. Your support and affirmation for your students' efforts and progress are vital, especially if they struggle initially. Your enthusiasm for the procedure as an effective learning tool will be contagious.

Your students' mind-maps do not have to be uniform. Key information should be recorded and linked so that it makes sense, but there should be latitude. With some classes, it may be appropriate to have all students map the information in the same way until they understand the method and can use it with facility. It's important, however, to encourage each student to develop his or her own creative style and individualized flair. The goals are to

- Make mind-mapping interesting and enjoyable.
- Help students develop increased academic self-confidence.
- Provide students with a resource they value and will *want* to use.

If you observe that certain students (or the entire class) are confused about how to connect the data or are struggling to comprehend the content of the material they're reading, you may need to review and reinforce the procedure using another facsimile textbook unit or article. You might model mind-mapping this unit at the chalkboard and methodically "spell out" the threads that link the ideas and data. Once students recognize how to make the key connections, their comprehension and recall should improve. A third option for classes with deficient reading comprehension skills is to begin mind-mapping a less challenging unit taken from a textbook that the students are currently using.

Having a visual image of important information and perceiving how data relate to other data can be an important memory catalyst. This is especially true in the case of students who are "natural" visual learners but who haven't discovered their natural facility on their own. Experimenting with mind-mapping can literally be an "eye opener" and help students appreciate talents they didn't realize they possessed. Remind students to abbreviate whenever possible but stress that they must be able to "read" their own mind-map! Students should place their completed mind-map in the appropriate section in their binder for future reference.

It's recommended that you also encourage your students to verbalize what they've included in their mind-maps. You could erase the model mind-map on the chalkboard and then go around the class and have students look at their own mind-maps and orally add facts and information to what has already been expressed by classmates. This procedure not only requires that students concentrate intently on what's being said in class, it also provides an opportunity for auditory learners to capitalize on their preferred learning modality. Oral recitation can be a powerful study and learning tool for auditory learners.

Expanding and Revising Your Mind-Map

In Step 5 of the mind-mapping method, students reread the unit, and, if appropriate expand, modify, and possibly redo their mind-maps. After they reread the unit, encourage them to add any important facts to their mind-maps that they've left out.

In Step 6, students practice distilling and summarizing in writing what they've learned. This procedure enhances reading comprehension and retention. Urge students to use their mind-maps to answer the main idea question they posed before reading the facsimile history unit, but discourage them from referring back to the article. You want them to realize how much they've learned about the Hundred Years' War by creating their mind-maps. You also want them to discover that mind-mapping can make studying more enjoyable and productive.

Reviewing the Mind-Mapping Steps

This exercise provides a quick review of the mind-mapping steps. Please note that your students will use "The Hundred Years' War" again in Unit 7, and they'll learn a great deal more about the subject matter when they learn, practice, and master the "Chewing-Up-Information" system. Don't expect their answers to the main idea question to be complete at this juncture. The primary goal is to have students write a cogent short essay that presents an overview of what they've learned so far. A secondary goal is to build your students' confidence in their written expressive language skills. In subsequent units, they'll have many additional opportunities to practice writing essays and improve their language arts skills. They'll also learn how to write powerful topic and concluding sentences and to organize their essays.

Answers to Quiz on Page 143

Quiz Answer Key: 1. *D* 2. *T* 3. *F* 4. *F* 5. *F* 6. *T* 7. *Bubonic plague* 8. *C* 9. *B* 10. *Great Schism* 11. *C* 12. *1346* 13. *F* 14. *F* 15. *Black Prince* 16. *Agincourt* 17. *Troyes* 18. *Joan of Arc* 19. *F* 20. *T*

Unit 6

Power Reading

For Students

LEARNING TO READ WITH MUSCLE

As he began to study the chapter about the Hundred Years' War in his European history textbook, Jason was already feeling anxious. He realized that the chapter test he would have to take in two weeks might determine whether he received an A− or a B+ on his report card. If he did well on the exam and received a good grade on the final, he would get the A− in the course. Getting the A− was very important to Jason because he desperately wanted this grade to raise his GPA and improve his chances of being accepted at his first choice college.

Jason's older brother, Jeremy, was a sophomore at UCLA. On his last visit home, he taught Jason a powerful study system that he claimed would help him identify, understand, and remember important information when he was studying. Jeremy called the method "mind-mapping," and he was convinced that it had played a big role in helping him get good grades in his college courses. Because Jeremy was a straight-A student, Jason was willing to give mind-mapping a try. Using a unit from Jason's science textbook, his brother carefully explained and demonstrated each step in the procedure.

After going through the procedure with his brother, Jason concluded that mind-mapping was easy and fun. It also allowed him to be creative. This really appealed to Jason. Before he headed back to college, Jeremy wrote down each of the mind-mapping steps for his brother. Jason realized that the history assignment offered an excellent opportunity for him to use mind-mapping. He pulled his brother's summary of the steps from his desk drawer and carefully reviewed them. He then took out a box of colored felt markers. His plan was to identify each key fact from the assigned unit, write it down on a piece of unlined paper, draw artistic designs around each fact, and connect the facts with lines or arrows. Jeremy had explained to him that this methodical procedure of creating a graphic representation of the information and connecting the data would help him better understand and recall the information.

Step 1 of the mind-mapping system was to read the title of the unit and to turn the title into a question using one of the three **main idea question words: *how, why*,** and ***what***. Jeremy had explained that asking a main idea question before you actually read the material helps to focus your mind on the content and stimulate your curiosity.

Jason looked at the title of the history unit. It was titled "The Hundred Years' War." Turning the title into a question was easy. Jason referred to the three main idea questions words. He realized that only two question words would make sense: "what" or "why." Jason chose "what" and asked the question, "What Was the Hundred Years' War?"

In *Step 2*, Jason reviewed in his mind what he already knew about the topic. Jason chuckled when he realized that he actually knew nothing about the Hundred Years' War, although somewhere in the back of his mind, he dimly recalled that the war had been fought during the Middle Ages.

Step 3 consisted of two parts. First he was supposed to speed-read the material very quickly without trying to pick out key facts. Jeremy had told him that the purpose of speed-reading the first time was simply to get an overview of the content. He also explained that when you speed-read, you don't read *every* word, but force your eyes to skim each line. Jeremy had showed Jason how to use his fingers like a moveable shutter to scan lines quickly (see page 117). He told Jason not to worry about pronouncing each word in his mind. After he finished his first scan of the material, Jason was to speed read the material again looking for "clumps" of information. This second scan was also supposed to be very rapid.

Speed-reading the eight pages in his textbook took only four minutes. Jeremy had told Jason not to be concerned if he couldn't recall a great deal of specific information, but it still seemed strange and a bit unsettling to read so quickly without being concerned about remembering all the facts. Then Jason speed-read the material a second time. This also took approximately four minutes. As Jeremy had warned, Jason still didn't remember very much, but he did have a somewhat better idea about what the material was about.

It was now time to "mind-map." Jason wrote the main idea question he had made from the title of the history unit: "WHAT WAS THE HUNDRED YEARS' WAR?" He wrote the question in capital letters in the middle of an unlined paper piece of paper that he had turned to a horizontal position. He then taped a second piece of paper to the first page and turn the paper over so that the tape was on the bottom. This provided more room to record and connect the important facts. Selecting a red felt-tipped colored marker, he drew a creative design around the question.

Jason was now ready to read the material carefully and slowly. In fact, his curiosity was aroused, and he was actually eager to read the unit. He wasn't satisfied with just having an overview of the content. He wanted to learn more.

Choosing different-colored markers to record each fact or chunk of information, Jason began reading the unit carefully. When he identified an important fact, he recorded it on his mind-map and drew creative circles and boxes around it. As he proceeded, he drew lines to connect this information to the title question in the middle of his paper. He also drew lines to connect related facts together. Jason was astonished by how much easier it was to understand, assimilate, and recall the information using the mind-mapping system. Everything seemed to make sense and fit together. The mind-map made the key facts easy to find and easy to understand. He could access all of the facts about the Hundred Years' War very quickly, and he was surprised by how much he was actually able to remember after doing his mind-map.

History had always been Jason's most challenging subject in school. Now studying for a history test didn't seem anywhere near as intimidating as it once did, and Jason discovered that reading about a war that happened during the Middle Ages was actually enjoyable. Score one for mind-mapping!

EXAMINING THE STORY

How would you evaluate Jason's willingness to accept his brother's suggestions?

1	2	3	4	5	6	7	8	9	10
Not Smart			**Fairly Smart**				**Very Smart**		

How would you evaluate the mind-mapping method that Jeremy showed Jason?

1	2	3	4	5	6	7	8	9	10
Not Smart			**Fairly Smart**				**Very Smart**		

How would you evaluate Jason's motivation, diligence, and effort?

1	2	3	4	5	6	7	8	9	10
Poor			**Average**				**Excellent**		

How would you evaluate Jason's ability to think strategically?

1	2	3	4	5	6	7	8	9	10
Poor			**Average**				**Excellent**		

Based on the description of Jason's study plan, make the following predictions.

How would you rate his chances of getting a B+ or an A− in his history course?

1	2	3	4	5	6	7	8	9	10
Poor			**Fair**				**Excellent**		

How likely is it that Jason will use the mind-mapping method in other classes?

1	2	3	4	5	6	7	8	9	10
Very Unlikely			**Fairly Likely**				**Very Likely**		

How would you rate Jason's chances being accepted at his first-choice college?

1	2	3	4	5	6	7	8	9	10
Very Unlikely			**Fairly Likely**				**Very Likely**		

Why did you make the preceding predictions?

_____

_____

_____

_____

_____

THINKING ABOUT WHAT YOU READ AND STUDY

You're now going to read the European history unit that Jason had to study for the test, and you're going to practice the first three steps of the mind-mapping procedure. Before you begin, take a moment to read and carefully consider the following "message."

A Message About "Boring" Material

You may not be particularly interested in learning about a war that happened almost seven hundred years ago, especially if you don't like history or lack confidence in your ability to understand material in history textbooks.

Throughout your education you can expect to encounter information that you find uninteresting. You must nonetheless learn this information to get good grades. The study methods you're going to practice will make the challenge of studying content you find boring less painful and less difficult. Knowing you can do well even on tests covering material you find uninteresting will build your academic self-confidence. You'll know you can study successfully no matter what the content. You may have to work hard to assimilate the content of this unit, but it's only through "stretching" that we develop our full range of abilities. Any professional athlete will confirm this. The true test of character is how we handle the tough situations, and not how we handle easy, comfortable ones. This character trait is often referred to as "having grit."

THE HUNDRED YEARS' WAR

Step 1: Turn the title into a **main idea question** using one of the main idea question words: **how, why, what**.

Question: _____?

[Hint: "Why Was There a Hundred Years' War?" or "What Was the Hundred Years' War?" You'll have many more opportunities to practice turning titles into questions in the next unit.]

Step 2: Write down anything you already know about the subject before reading the material. (You may actually know something about the Hundred Years' War. Perhaps you saw the movie *Time Line*, which dealt with a battle that was fought during the war. Of course, some of the content in the movie was fictionalized. If you know nothing about the topic, leave the following section blank.)

WHAT I ALREADY KNOW ABOUT THIS SUBJECT

_____

_____

_____

_____

_____

SPEED-READING: SKIMMING FOR INFORMATION

It's time to speed-read the Hundred Years' War unit. Notice in the following illustration how the fingers form a "shutter." By using your fingers in this way and moving them rapidly, you can skim or scan words quickly and easily, without reading or pronouncing each word in your mind.

The war, which 1337 d ended in 1453, was
actually a se cts that were

Moving your fingers *quickly* across each line from left to right will help you speed-read. *Resist the temptation to read each word carefully and to pronounce it in your mind.* At first, you may find this challenging, because this is not the way you were taught to read in elementary school. Speed-reading is a very different skill. It's simply a tool you can use to get an overview when you first begin to read or study something new. In other situations, you'll still need to read the material carefully and accurately.

Step 3: Speed-read the material. Spend no more than **4 minutes** scanning or skimming the material. *Remember:* You are not expected to remember a great deal of information when you speed-read. You simply want to get an overview of the content. Forcing yourself to scan material quickly will probably be difficult at first because you're not used to the technique. With practice, the procedure will become easy!

THE HUNDRED YEARS' WAR

Imagine a war between two countries that lasts for more than one hundred years. Then imagine a war in which you, your father, you grandfather, your great grandfather, your great, great grandfather, and your great, great, great grandfather all have fought. This would mean six generations of your family fighting in the same war against the same enemy. Wouldn't that be astounding? Well, such a war actually happened during the Middle Ages. It was called the Hundred Years' War.

The war between France and England began in 1337 and ended 1453. During the 116 years that this seemingly never-ending conflict lasted, a succession of five English and five French kings fought for control of France. Because occasional truces and treaties temporarily interrupted the fighting, the war was really a series of wars. The truces, however, were repeatedly broken and the treaties repeatedly discarded; thus two of the most powerful countries in Europe remained locked in an ongoing battle for more than a century.

Social Conditions in the Middle Ages

The Middle Ages (or medieval times) lasted from A.D. 500 to 1500. During this period, there was great social turmoil. By the 1300s, feudalism—a system in which great hereditary landowners owned the land and demanded payment and absolute loyalty from peasants working on it—had begun to break down. The power structure shifted, and the feudal lords lost much of their authority. This transformation significantly altered the fabric of medieval society.

While these changes were occurring, the economies of Europe were recovering from a period of decreasing population, social discontent, and shrinking industry and trade. Enriched by this economic improvement, the kings hired armies to enforce their power over the lords. Using new battle strategies and tactics, their well-equipped infantry outmatched the weaker armies of the feudal knights and repeatedly defeated them.

The Hundred Years' War interrupted the economic recovery. The continuous conflict between France and England damaged trade and weakened the economies of both countries. At the same time, the war hastened the breakdown of feudalism and fueled the civil wars that were spreading throughout Europe. Peasants rose in bloody revolts against the lords. Workers in towns clashed with the merchants who denied them a decent wage and kept them powerless.

The Black Death

The misery suffered by the people was made worse by a gruesome epidemic called the bubonic plague. This epidemic was referred to at the time as the Black Death because black spots of dried blood could be seen under the skin of its victims. The disease was spread to humans by fleas that infested the millions of infected rats that thrived in a society where good sanitation and personal hygiene were essentially nonexistent. These unhygienic conditions produced an ideal environment for the bubonic plague to spread. Between 1347 and 1352, the Black Death destroyed twenty-five percent of the population of Europe. Severe droughts and floods added to the miseries of the people and brought famine and other diseases.

Despite these terrible conditions, the kings were able to increase their power by winning the support of the middle class that comprised merchants who lived in towns. These merchants wanted peace and stable government and were willing to support the kings and pay taxes in return for social order and stability.

The Role of the Church

As the power of the kings increased, so, too, did the power of the church and the popes. In both France and England, priests, bishops, and cardinals had great influence on political affairs during the Middle Ages. To keep the church in check, the kings interfered in church affairs and, occasionally, they were successful in controlling the popes and forcing them to surrender their independence. This was especially true during the period from 1309 to 1377 when popes resided in Avignon and ruled the church from France. Later, when the papacy returned to Rome, there were great divisions within the church about how the popes were elected. This period of turmoil in the church was called the *Great Schism* and lasted from 1378 to 1417. At times, two and, in some cases, three prelates claimed to be pope concurrently. These religious conflicts seriously undermined the influence of the church and its teachings and were one of the factors that ultimately led to the Protestant Reformation in the 1500s.

The War Begins

During the Middle Ages, the English and French royal families often intermarried and shared common ancestors. When the French king Charles IV died in 1328 without a male heir, his cousin Philip IV assumed the throne and began a new dynasty. In 1337, King Edward III of England, who was Charles IV's nephew, claimed the French throne, and this demand was the fuse that ignited the Hundred Years' War.

The war began when King Philip VI of France declared that he would take over a region called Guyenne. King Edward III of England refused to allow King Philip to follow through on his planned annexation of the region. King Edward claimed the French throne for himself, basing his entitlement on the fact that his mother was the sister of three French kings.

The English army was about one-third the size of the French army. Despite being considerable outnumbered, the English won most the battles because of superior military tactics. The French, however, actually ended up winning the war.

The Major Battles

The first important battle of the Hundred Years' War was fought at Crécy in 1346. King Edward III's brilliant victory over the French in this battle was attributable to the skills of the English infantry and archers. The English archers used longbows that had a rate of fire six times that of the crossbows used by the French, and this weapon played a major role in their victory.

The English also benefited from social upheaval in France that lead to uprisings in Flanders in 1338, Brittany in 1341, and Normandy in 1355.

King Edward III's son, who was called the Black Prince, led the English army in their next great victory in the Battle of Poitiers in 1356. This battle ended with the Treaty of Bretigny in 1360 and produced a brief period of peace.

Despite England's victories, the English people began to oppose the never-ending war. The Parliament (the English legislature) refused to approve the taxes that were required to sustain the war effort. A peasant's revolt against forced labor and high taxes broke out in 1381, but King Richard II, the son of the Black Prince, put down the rebellion. Later, Richard tried to undermine the power of Parliament. He proved to be an incompetent king, however, and in 1399, he was forced to give up the throne. His rival, the duke of Lancaster, was chosen by Parliament to replace him, and he became Henry IV. Preoccupied with fighting wars against the English nobles, King Henry IV paid little attention to France. His eldest son, Henry, became King Henry V in 1413, and he renewed the war with France.

Setting aside the treaty of Bretigny, Henry V was determined to follow through on Edward III's claim to the French throne. Henry was renowned for his military skills and under his leadership, the English were once again triumphant in 1415 at the Battle of Agincourt. The English army comprised only 6,000 men. Its highly disciplined archers supported by cavalry were able to defeat the much larger French army, which consisted of 20,000 to 30,000 men. This battle marked the third major English victory in the Hundred Years' War. The English then went on to conquer all of Normandy.

In 1420, the Treaty of Troyes declared that the English king, Henry V, was the regent (ruler in place of the king) and heir to the French throne. Henry then married the daughter of his enemy Charles VI of France. After Henry V died in 1422, the French refused to accept the English claim to the throne. War broke out again, and during the next six years, the English swept through northern France. In 1429, the French forces led by a peasant woman named Joan of Arc defeated the English army in the Battle of Orleans. Imprisoned by the English, Joan of Arc was later burned at the stake. More French victories followed, and by the time the Hundred Years' War ended in 1453, the English controlled only the French city of Calais. Because King Henry V's son, Henry VI, was unable to hold onto the conquered French territory, he was overthrown. Calais was ultimately recaptured by the French in 1558, and the English were finally forced to return to their island on the other side of the English Channel.

The Hundred Years' War profoundly influenced European history at the end of the Middle Ages. It had a significant effect on French and English society. The nobility and centralized governments in both countries were weakened. French unity was strengthened. New military tactics were developed. The power and influence of the English navy increased. New geographic boundaries were established. England and France were finally separate and distinct.[1]

Time Line for Hundred Years' War
Major Events

Hundred Years' War
Major Events Timeline

1328	1337	1346	1356	1360	1381
King Charles IV dies Philip IV becomes king	King Edward III (E.) claims French throne	Battle of Crécy English victory	Battle of Poitiers English victory by Black Prince	Treaty of Bretigny Brief peace	Rebellion in England put down by King Richard II

1399	1415	1420	1422	1428	1429
King Richard II forced to abdicate Henry IV becomes king	Battle of Agincourt English victory	Treaty of Troyes King Henry V (E) regent of France	King Henry V dies King Henry VI crowned War breaks out again	English occupy northern France	Battle of Orleans French victory led by Joan of Arc

---

1. Sources: *World Book* and *Encyclopedia Britannica*.

PRACTICING MIND-MAPPING

Mini Mind-Map: The Introduction
to the Hundred Years' War Unit

Unit 6
Art for Mind-Map for Introduction to 100 Years' War Unit

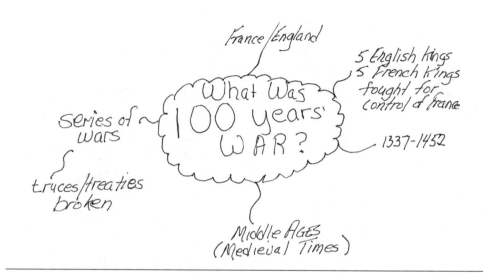

Step 4: Mind-map the material. You're about to become an artist! **You'll need colored pencils or felt pens to complete Step 4.** On a separate piece of unlined paper that you've turned horizontally, use one of your colored pens or pencils to write the main idea question, "What Was The Hundred Years' War?" in the center of the page. Be as creative as you want making designs around any of the information you write down. Use colors you like. (You may also choose not to make designs or to use colored pens or pencils. You may also prefer to simply use a pencil. This is perfectly OK. Using colors and making designs is intended to make the project fun and could improve your ability to recall the information.) Write relatively small so you can fit the information on the paper. Include only the **key** ideas in your mind-map. Leave out unnecessary words. **If you conclude that you can't fit everything on one page, tape together two pieces of unlined paper.** Plan ahead so that you have enough room to draw the arrows and boxes. Draw lines to show how the information you're recording is linked to other information and to the unit title.

COMPARING MIND-MAPS

Look at the completed mind-map that follows. Compare what's been included in the model mind-map with what you've included. *Your mind-map does not necessarily have to look like this, but it should contain most of the information in the sample.* If you've left key data out, think about why this information is important and why your teacher might want you to understand and recall it.

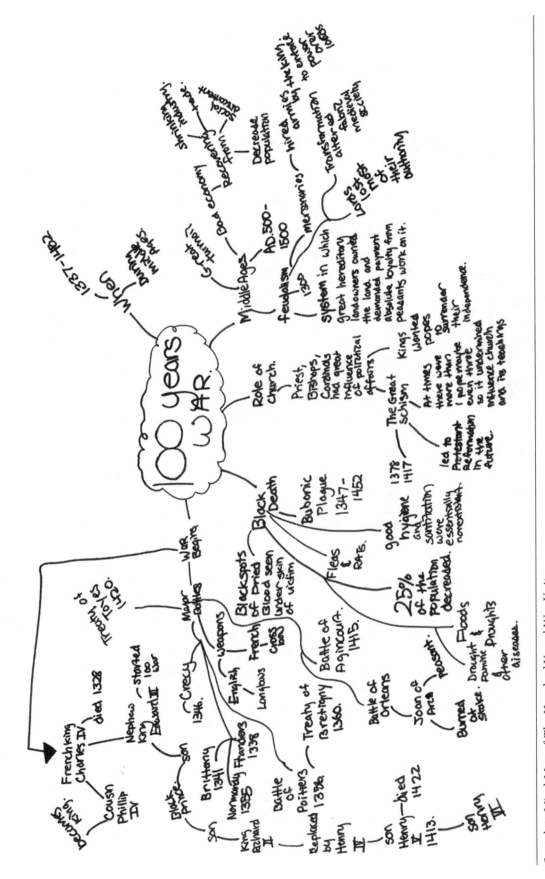

Complete Mind-Map of The Hundred Years' War Unit

Source: Drawn by Oneill Kim, age 15.

EXPANDING AND REVISING YOUR MIND-MAP

Step 5: Reread the unit, and, if appropriate expand, modify, and possibly redo your mind-map. As you reread the unit, you may want to add important facts to your mind-map that you have left out. Redoing your mind-map is time-consuming, but the process will help you better understand and recall the information. With practice, you will "get it right" the first time, and you won't need to make revisions. You can, thus, eliminate Step 5. If you do decide to alter or add significantly to your mind-map, draw your revised or expanded mind-map below or on a separate sheet of three-hole punched, unlined paper. Place your expanded mind-map in your binder for future reference.

Your Revised/Expanded Mind-map

Step 6: Answer the Title Question. Using your mind-map, write a paragraph that answers the main idea question you posed before you began reading the unit. Begin your paragraph with a powerful topic sentence and include in the answer the information in your mind-map. You may use the following sample topic sentence to begin your essay, or you may prefer to make up your own. Once you choose a topic sentence, incorporate into your essay the facts and data that succinctly summarizes the key information about the Hundred Years' War.

Sample Topic Sentence

The Hundred Years' War, which lasted from 1337 to 1453, profoundly shaped European history at the end of the Middle Ages.

What Was the Hundred Years' War?

_____

_____

_____

_____

_____

_____

_____

_____

_____

_____

REVIEWING THE MIND-MAPPING STEPS

Number the following mind-mapping steps in the proper order.

Step _____ : **Answer title question.**

Step _____ : **Write down everything you know about the subject before reading the material.**

Step _____ : **Turn the title into a main idea question.**

Step _____ : **Read the material carefully and slowly and mind-map.**

Step _____ : **Speed-read the material.**

Step _____ : **Expand or redo mind-map.**

You may wish to continue using mind-mapping as a learning and studying tool whenever you have to extract and assimilate information in your text-books. In the next two units, you'll learn and practice other ways to record information, and you'll be able to select the method or combination of methods that work best for you.

Unit 7

Reading Comprehension at Warp Speed

For Teachers

Objectives

This unit introduces a powerful, easy-to-use methodology for enhancing students' reading comprehension, information recall, expository writing, and summarization skills.

LESSON PLAN

1. Students read **Something Went Very Wrong** and discuss Lauren's options after receiving an unexpected poor grade on a test. They assess her possible responses to the setback and explain their rationales.

2. In **Reading: More Than Just Words**, students consider how their brain assimilates information when they read. The discussion segues to the introduction of a comprehensive five-step study method called the **"Chewing-Up-Information"** system.

OVERCOMING INTELLECTUAL PASSIVITY

Many underperforming students actually spend a great deal of time doing homework and studying. They may work diligently, but at the same time they work ineffectually and derive marginal benefits from their efforts. These underachieving students haven't learned how to identify, comprehend, and assimilate key information when they study, a phenomenon directly attributable to passive learning. The outcome of their intellectual disengagement when they attempt to absorb information is predictable: marginal comprehension, deficient retention of essential data, poor grades, and reduced academic self-confidence.

Intellectual passivity is habit forming. Students who are chronically disconnected intellectually when they read and study are predisposed to becoming cerebrally "anesthetized." Doing little more than going through the motions of studying, they fail to recognize a basic scholastic fact of life: Academic achievement requires intense, dynamic, and focused participation in the learning process.

The pedagogical antidote for passive learning is to provide students with an accessible and functional method for "digesting" information so that it can be understood and assimilated. Students must be trained to ask incisive questions when they read and study. They must also be taught how to identify important information and how use this information to answer not only their own questions, but also the ones that their teachers are likely to ask on the next test.

DEALING WITH TRANSPARENT EXCUSES AND RATIONALIZATIONS

When confronted with academic setbacks, many ineffectual learners become intent on defending themselves or blaming others for their plight. The litany of excuses and justifications typically includes the following:

- "The test was unfair!"
- "I never do well on multiple-choice tests!"
- "The questions didn't cover what we were supposed to study!"
- "A lot of my answers were right, but the teacher marked them wrong!"
- "The course is stupid and boring."

These transparent excuses are clearly self-serving and self-protecting. By blaming and complaining about perceived injustices, students who resort to these excuses and rationalizations are obviously trying to absolve themselves of responsibility for their inadequate performance, and, in many cases, their inadequate effort.

Being upset when you do poorly on a test and having your self-confidence temporarily shaken are understandable reactions to a setback. Smart students (i.e., those who are capable of *thinking strategically*) are usually able to bounce back from these reversals. They analyze what went wrong and make the requisite strategic and tactical adjustments to prevent a recurrence of the debacle.

For example, if their grade on a science test clearly reveals that they didn't understand key information, strategically minded students will make certain that they do a better job of identifying and assimilating what's important when they study for the next test.

Students who have an extended track record of poor academic performance are especially vulnerable to scholastic setbacks. Their chronic marginal performance can damage their emotional resiliency and cause them to become demoralized and resigned. To protect themselves, many of these students will simply lower the expectations and aspirations. A light glimmers at the end of this dreary tunnel, however. Once students acquire more productive study skills and begin to achieve in school, their self-confidence and emotional resiliency will usually improve. They will be less defensive and less prone to making excuses. Success is a powerful antidote for a bruised ego.

SUMMARY OF STUDENT EXERCISES AND ACTIVITIES

Examining the Story

In this exercise, students examine a case study about a highly motivated, goal-directed teenager who receives a poor grade on a test. They then methodically analyze the protagonist's possible responses to this unanticipated disappointment. Because most teenagers have experienced similar scholastic reversals at one time or another, they should readily relate to this anecdote.

Students discuss Lauren's three basic options for responding to her poor grade, and they examine the associated emotions. They then evaluate the wisdom of each option and make predictions about the potential repercussions. The intent of the activity is to encourage students to analyze their own setbacks rationally and constructively and to discourage them from becoming demoralized and resigned to failure.

After evaluating the protagonist's options, students explore how Lauren might avoid a similar debacle in the future. The objective is for students to assimilate a critically important cause-and-effect principle—namely, that smart students carefully analyze their setbacks, evaluate their possible responses to the situation, consider the potential consequences of their choices, and then proactively do what needs to be done to resolve the problem.

Students are guided to a key insight: Before Lauren can develop a more effective study strategy, she must first identify the reasons why she did poorly on the test. Once she pinpoints the underlying causes, she can then make the appropriate expedient revisions in her study plan.

Reading: More Than Just Words

Students consider what happens to information that enters their brain when they study. For many students, this may be the first time they've ever thought about how their mind actually functions when they are reading and studying.

The "Chewing-Up-Information" System

Successful students realize that to study effectively, they must think about what's important, what the words they're reading mean, and what they must understand, assimilate, and retain. The **Chewing-Up-Information** system trains them to ask probing questions about the content of what they're studying and methodically teaches them how to identify the important information they must comprehend and recall to get good grades.

Chewing-Up-Information Steps

Step 1: Turn the title into a question using a main idea question word.

Step 2: Speed read the material.

Step 3: Turn each subtitle into a question.

Step 4: Reread the material and highlight or underline information.

Step 5: Answer subtitle questions and title questions.

Explanation

Step 1: Students turn the title into a main idea question. This step is the same as Step 1 of the mind-mapping method. Students are taught to differentiate **main idea** from **detail** question words. They practice using main idea question words to turn subheadings in the Hundred Years' War unit into main idea questions. To reinforce mastery, they also practice the converse and turn questions into subheadings.

Step 2: Students turn each subtitle of the Hundred Years' War unit into main idea questions. (Please refer to student content.)

Step 3: Students speed-read the unit a second time. (This step is the same as Step 3 in the **mind-mapping method.**)

Step 4: At this juncture, the mind-mapping method and Chewing-Up-Information system diverge. Instead of graphically representing key information, students practice highlighting this information as a precursor to standard note taking. (*Please note:* Students are explicitly instructed *not* to underline or highlight in their textbooks. In Unit 8, they'll learn how to take textbook notes without underscoring or highlighting.) During a class discussion, students examine the modeled underlined information in paragraphs 1–3. Once they understand the concept of identifying important information, they practice highlighting or underlining key ideas in the facsimile unit. This is a antecedent to learning how to take traditional notes, which is introduced in the next unit.

You may want to have your students examine and discuss their highlighting of the key information in small cooperative study groups. These groups should be heterogeneous, comprising students who scored well on the test and those who had difficulty with it. Students should present their reasons for highlighting particular information. If they conclude that they omitted important data when they highlighted, urge them to make appropriate additions. You might also initiate a class discussion about the need to be deliberately focused and vigilant when targeting key information.

Step 5: Students now answer the subtitle questions they posed in **Step 2**. (They've already answered the main idea question in Unit 6.) They should be allowed to use both their mind-map and the highlighted information to answer these questions. They then take a practice quiz that will ideally demonstrate how much they've learned using the mind-mapping and Chewing-Up-Information methods. Students then critically examine their scores on the quiz. The objective is to demonstrate that when mind-mapping and the **Chewing-Up-Information** system are used either independently or in tandem, they provide powerful and highly effective study resources.

Students systematically practice each step in the study system. After they learn the first four steps, they use the system with the reproduced Hundred Years' War unit. To reinforce mastery, it's recommended that they then apply the method in studying material from one of their own textbooks.

Encouraging students to underline or highlight in their workbook can, of course, be risky because they might construe this as permission to highlight their regular textbooks. The goal of the highlighting and underlining procedure is to demonstrate how to identify key data when reading. As stated earlier, the procedure is a precursor to taking traditional notes directly from textbooks and is used to illustrate how to target important information. Students should be told that highlighting is permitted only on these worksheets. In Unit 8, students learn how to transfer the key information directly to their notes without having to mark their textbooks.

You can significantly reduce resistance to the Chewing-Up-Information system if you help your students recognize that although the system will probably require additional study time, it will produce better grades because their studying will be far more focused and efficient. Be prepared to provide extra help and supervision for students with deficient academic skills and diminished self-confidence. As the study and analytical thinking skills of these students improve, their perceptions about their abilities should undergo a gradual transformation. Before these positive changes in attitude and self-perception can realistically occur, students will require concrete evidence that they're making progress and are actually capable of achieving academically. Once their grades begin to reflect their improved study skills, their motivation and effort should improve commensurately.

Answering Subtitle Questions

Students must not only develop the ability to ask incisive questions about what they're reading, they must also be able to answer the questions they pose effectively and succinctly. The acquisition of first-rate expository writing and summarization skills hinges on students' comprehending what they've read and on their being able to communicate their understanding. If students are to improve their language arts skills, they must practice expository writing extensively, and they must be provided with feedback. Students should be encouraged to discuss their answers to the subtitle questions in class or in small cooperative study groups, and they should be encouraged to revise and edit their answers when appropriate. It goes without saying that the feedback they receive from you and their classmates should be tempered, especially if they are struggling to express their ideas in writing. The goals are for them to establish the habit of objectively critiquing their own work and for them to improve their ability to summarize and distill information.

Quiz on the Hundred Years' War

Ideally, this quiz will demonstrate to students that the Chewing-Up-Information system has helped them learn a great deal about the Hundred Years' War. Some students will undoubtedly find certain questions on the test difficult. You want to encourage your students to use logic to eliminate as many incorrect answers as possible when they are taking a multiple-choice test. To practice this procedure, it's recommended that you select specific questions on the quiz and model how logic can be applied to eliminate answers that are clearly incorrect.

Examining Your Performance on the Quiz

Students who do poorly on the quiz should be reassured that their test performance will improve if they continue to use the Chewing-Up-Information system and study diligently. They should also be apprised that other powerful study techniques will be introduced in subsequent units.

Students with low test scores should be given an opportunity to retake the quiz. The goal is ideally to furnish students with tangible evidence that they have improved their comprehension, study efficacy, and test performance. This improvement will be a major confidence builder. Once students become convinced the Chewing-Up-Information system can actually produce better grades, they will be far more receptive to using the system.

Reviewing the Chewing-Up-Information System and Questions About Studying

These brief exercises are designed to recap and reinforce what students have learned about studying productively.

Unit 7

Reading Comprehension at Warp Speed

For Students

SOMETHING WENT VERY WRONG

Lauren had her heart set on getting an A on the history final. She had studied very hard, and she was convinced that she knew the material backward and forward. The eleventh-grader felt that she deserved an A.

As she waited for the test to be handed out, Lauren felt calm and confident. She imagined her teacher handing back the test the following day with a red A at the top. She also imagined how pleased her parents would be when she showed them her grade. According to her calculations, an A on the final would guarantee an A in the course. This would raise her GPA to 3.5, and this was important because she realized that she would need a minimum 3.5 GPA to get a scholarship to the university she wanted to attend.

When the teacher finally handed out the test, Lauren felt a sense of relief. "Let's get this over with," she thought. After quickly scanning the questions, Laura's sense of relief turned to panic. She felt fear surge through her body. It was as if she were looking at a test covering material she had never seen before! Her panic accelerated. She didn't think she could answer more than 50 percent of the questions! The more upset she became, the more she seemed to forget.

When Lauren handed in the test forty minutes later, she felt she would be lucky to get a C–. Badly shaken and depressed, she quickly left the room when the bell rang. Her fantasy of getting an A on the final exam and an A in the course had shattered, and she was devastated.

EXAMINING THE STORY

No one can accuse Lauren of being irresponsible or lazy. She had established her goal for the test, and she had prepared conscientiously. After having spent hours studying, she felt confident about doing well on the test. Then something unexpected happened: Lauren discovered she wasn't as well prepared as she thought! There are four likely explanations for what happened:

1. She hadn't learned the information as adequately as she had thought.

2. She hadn't accurately identified what her teacher considered important.

3. She was surprised by the types of questions that were asked on the exam.

4. She panicked during the test and couldn't recall what she had studied.

Any one of these factors could have caused the disaster.

You, too, may have experienced a similar "nightmare." You studied conscientiously, and you were confident you would hit a "home run" on a test. Then your teacher threw you a "curveball" that you didn't expect. Perhaps you studied the wrong material, or perhaps you couldn't remember key information that you thought you knew.

Everyone occasionally miscalculates, and *everyone* occasionally suffers a disappointment or a setback in school. A key characteristic, however, distinguishes students who think smart from those who don't. When faced with a setback, kids who use their heads don't beat themselves up, and they don't come "unglued." Rather than fall apart, they bounce back from the setback. They identify what went wrong and figure out how to deal with the situation. They also learn from their mistake and do everything possible to make sure that they don't repeat it.

Imagine that you did poorly on a test because you studied the wrong material or forgot to include important information in an essay question. If you're thinking smart, you'll analyze the problem, identify the mistakes, and make the necessary adjustments in your study or test-taking strategy. Instead of giving up, becoming depressed, or mindlessly repeating the same miscalculations, you deliberately develop a better plan. This calculated thinking and persistence in response to a defeat is often described as "grit" and "having character."

When Lauren "blew" the test, she was at a crossroads. She had to decide how to respond to the disappointment. She had several options.

Option 1: She could lower her expectations and resign herself to doing poorly on history tests no matter how hard she studied.

Probable consequence: Frustration, loss of confidence and pride, depression, and continued low grades.

Option 2: She could continue to use the same study strategy and hope for the best next time.

Probable consequence: Low grades, frustration, reduced self-confidence, and loss of pride.

Option 3: She could identify the reasons she did poorly on the test and make tactical adjustments in her study strategy.

Probable consequence: Better grades, increased self-confidence and pride, elevated expectations, and improved motivation to continue studying.

If faced with a similar setback, which choice would you make? _____

If Lauren selects **Option 1,** evaluate this decision.

1	2	3	4	5	6	7	8	9	10
Not Smart			**Fairly Smart**				**Very Smart**		

Why did you make this evaluation?

_____

_____

If Lauren selects **Option 2,** evaluate this decision.

1	2	3	4	5	6	7	8	9	10
Not Smart			**Fairly Smart**				**Very Smart**		

Why did you make this evaluation?

_____

_____

If Lauren selects **Option 3,** evaluate this decision.

1	2	3	4	5	6	7	8	9	10
Not Smart			**Fairly Smart**				**Very Smart**		

Why did you make this evaluation?

_____

_____

READING: MORE THAN JUST WORDS

As you scanned the unit about the Hundred Years' War (Unit 6), your brain was absorbing information through your eyes. Like a TV signal, the words on the page were beamed directly to your brain. There your brain instantaneously linked the words with their meaning. For example, when you read the words "Middle Ages," your mind made an association with the definition of these words because they are familiar to you. Without realizing it, you may have actually formed a mental picture of a knight in armor on a magnificent black horse holding a large sword in one hand.

Later in the unit, you read the word "annexation." You may never have seen this word before. Although you might figure out the word from the context in which it is used, you would have to think more carefully about the word than you would about "Middle Ages." Let's say you looked up "annexation" in the dictionary. To remember the word and its definition *(adding on to),* you'd probably have to say it several times and link it with the word "add." You could remember the word better if you visualized in your mind a king's army defeating an enemy in battle and taking ownership the enemy's territory and annexing it. (This visual association method is examined in Unit 9.)

You may not realize it, but your mind continually receives signals from your eyes and ears. Functioning like a computer, your brain absorbs the information (if you're paying attention), "digests" it, and then tells you what to do with it. Under most conditions, your brain works quickly and effectively. For example, if someone asks you, "Who was the first president of the United States?" or "How much is 9×9?" you could recall the answers and respond immediately. If you were very sleepy, however, you brain would lose its efficiency and might not be able to recall, understand, and communicate information efficiently.

You've already learned a powerful method called mind-mapping that helps you understand and remember information. It's time to learn another method for using your brain's computer. It's called the **"Chewing-Up-Information"** system.

You may be wondering, "Why learn another method?" The answer is simple. If you practice several different techniques of studying effectively, you can choose the one that works best for you. You may also decide to combine parts of several methods and create your own personalized study system. To practice the Chewing-Up-Information system, you'll be using the Hundred Years' War unit again. *Don't reread the material now.* Skip ahead to page 138.

THE HUNDRED YEARS' WAR

Imagine a war between two countries that lasts for more than one hundred years. Then imagine a war in which you, your father, you grandfather, your great grandfather, your great, great grandfather, and your great, great, great grandfather all have fought. This would mean six generations of your family fighting in the same war against the same enemy. Wouldn't that be astounding? Well, such a war actually happened during the Middle Ages. It was called the Hundred Years' War.

The war between France and England began in 1337 and ended in 1453. During the 116 years that this seemingly never-ending conflict lasted, a succession of five English and five French kings fought for control of France. Because occasional truces and treaties temporarily interrupted the fighting, the war was really a series of wars. The truces, however, were repeatedly broken and the treaties repeatedly discarded; thus two of the most powerful countries in Europe remained locked in an ongoing battle for more than a century.

Social Conditions in the Middle Ages

The Middle Ages (or medieval times) lasted from A.D. 500 to 1500. During this period, there was great social turmoil. By the 1300s, feudalism—a system in which great hereditary landowners owned the land and demanded payment and absolute loyalty from peasants working on it—had begun to break down. The power structure shifted, and the feudal lords lost much of their authority. This transformation significantly altered the fabric of medieval society.

While these changes were occurring, the economies of Europe were recovering from a period of decreasing population, social discontent, and shrinking industry and trade. Enriched by this economic improvement, the kings hired armies to enforce their power over the lords. Using new battle strategies and tactics, their well-equipped infantry outmatched the weaker armies of the feudal knights and repeatedly defeated them.

The Hundred Years' War interrupted the economic recovery. The continuous conflict between France and England damaged trade and weakened the economies of both countries. At the same time, the war hastened the breakdown of feudalism and fueled the civil wars that were spreading throughout Europe. Peasants rose in bloody revolts against the lords. Workers in towns clashed with the merchants who denied them a decent wage and kept them powerless.

The Black Death

The misery suffered by the people was made worse by a gruesome epidemic called the bubonic plague. This epidemic was referred to at the time as the Black Death because black spots of dried blood could be seen under the skin of its victims. The disease was spread to humans by fleas that infested the millions of infected rats that thrived in a society where good sanitation and personal hygiene were essentially nonexistent. These unhygienic conditions produced an ideal environment for the bubonic plague to spread. Between 1347 and 1352, the Black Death destroyed twenty-five percent of the population of Europe. Severe droughts and floods added to the miseries of the people and brought famine and other diseases.

Despite these terrible conditions, the kings were able to increase their power by winning the support of the middle class that comprised merchants who lived in towns. These merchants wanted peace and stable government and were willing to support the kings and pay taxes in return for social order and stability.

The Role of the Church

As the power of the kings increased, so, too, did the power of the church and the popes. In both France and England, priests, bishops, and cardinals had great influence on political affairs during the Middle Ages. To keep the church in check, the kings interfered in church affairs and, occasionally, they were successful in controlling the popes and forcing them to surrender their independence. This was especially true during the period from 1309 to 1377 when popes resided in Avignon and ruled the church from France. Later, when the papacy returned to Rome, there were great divisions within the church about how the popes were elected. This period of turmoil in the church was called the *Great Schism* and lasted from 1378 to 1417. At times, two and, in some cases, three prelates claimed to be pope concurrently. These religious conflicts seriously undermined the influence of the church and its teachings and were one of the factors that ultimately led to the Protestant Reformation in the 1500s.

The War Begins

During the Middle Ages, the English and French royal families often intermarried and shared common ancestors. When the French king Charles IV died in 1328 without a male heir, his cousin Philip IV assumed the throne and began a new dynasty. In 1337, King Edward III of England, who was Charles IV's nephew, claimed the French throne, and this demand was the fuse that ignited the Hundred Years' War.

The war began when King Philip VI of France declared that he would take over a region called Guyenne. King Edward III of England refused to allow King Philip to follow through on his planned annexation of the region. King Edward claimed the French throne for himself, basing his entitlement on the fact that his mother was the sister of three French kings.

The English army was about one-third the size of the French army. Despite being considerable outnumbered, the English won most the battles because of superior military tactics. The French, however, actually ended up winning the war.

The Major Battles

The first important battle of the Hundred Years' War was fought at Crécy in 1346. King Edward III's brilliant victory over the French in this battle was attributable to the skills of the English infantry and archers. The English archers used longbows that had a rate of fire six times that of the crossbows used by the French, and this weapon played a major role in their victory.

The English also benefited from social upheaval in France that lead to uprisings in Flanders in 1338, Brittany in 1341, and Normandy in 1355.

King Edward III's son, who was called the Black Prince, led the English army in their next great victory in the Battle of Poitiers in 1356. This battle ended with the Treaty of Bretigny in 1360 and produced a brief period of peace.

Despite England's victories, the English people began to oppose the never-ending war. The Parliament (the English legislature) refused to approve the taxes that were required to sustain the war effort. A peasant's revolt against forced labor and high taxes broke out in 1381, but King Richard II, the son of the Black Prince, put down the rebellion. Later, Richard tried to undermine the power of Parliament. He proved to be an incompetent king, however, and in 1399, he was forced to give up the throne. His rival, the duke of Lancaster, was chosen by Parliament to replace him, and he became Henry IV. Preoccupied with fighting wars against the English nobles, King Henry IV paid little attention to France. His eldest son, Henry, became King Henry V in 1413, and he renewed the war with France.

Setting aside the treaty of Bretigny, Henry V was determined to follow through on Edward III's claim to the French throne. Henry was renowned for his military skills and under his leadership, the English were once again triumphant in 1415 at the Battle of Agincourt. The English army comprised only 6,000 men. Its highly disciplined archers supported by cavalry were able to defeat the much larger French army, which consisted of 20,000 to 30,000 men. This battle marked the third major English victory in the Hundred Years' War. The English then went on to conquer all of Normandy.

In 1420, the Treaty of Troyes declared that the English king, Henry V, was the regent (ruler in place of the king) and heir to the French throne. Henry then married the daughter of his enemy Charles VI of France. After Henry V died in 1422, the French refused to accept the English claim to the throne. War broke out again, and during the next six years, the English swept through northern France. In 1429, the French forces led by a peasant woman named Joan of Arc defeated the English army in the Battle of Orleans. Imprisoned by the English, Joan of Arc was later burned at the stake. More French victories followed, and by the time the Hundred Years' War ended in 1453, the English controlled only the French city of Calais. Because King Henry V's son, Henry VI, was unable to hold onto the conquered French territory, he was overthrown. Calais was ultimately recaptured by the French in 1558, and the English were finally forced to return to their island on the other side of the English Channel.

The Hundred Years' War profoundly influenced European history at the end of the Middle Ages. It had a significant effect on French and English society. The nobility and centralized governments in both countries were weakened. French unity was strengthened. New military tactics were developed. The power and influence of the English navy increased. New geographic boundaries were established. England and France were finally separate and distinct.[1]

Time Line for Hundred Years' War
Major Events

Hundred Years' War
Major Events Timeline

1328	1337	1346	1356	1360	1381
King Charles IV dies	King Edward III (E.)	Battle of Crécy	Battle of Poitiers	Treaty of Bretigny	Rebellion in England
Philip IV becomes	claims French throne	English victory	English victory by	Brief peace	put down by King
king			Black Prince		Richard II

1399	1415	1420	1422	1428	1429
King Richard II forced	Battle of Agincourt	Treaty of Troyes	King Henry V dies	English occupy	Battle of Orlean
to abdicate	English victory	King Henry V (E)	King Henry VI	northern France	French victory
Henry IV becomes king		regent of France	crowned		led by Joan of Arc
			War breaks out again		

1. Sources: *World Book* and *Encyclopedia Britannica*.

THE CHEWING-UP-INFORMATION SYSTEM

The **Chewing-Up-Information** system consists of **seven steps.** You will learn and practice four steps in this unit, and you will practice the remaining three steps in Unit 8.

Step 1: Turn the title into a question *before* scanning and reading the material. *(This step is the same as in the mind-mapping method.)*

Reason: Asking a question about what you are about to read before actually beginning to read helps you *think about* and *understand* the information.

Title: "The Hundred Years' War"

Question: *What Was the Hundred Years' War?* (You've actually already posed this question in Unit 6 before you began to mind-map.)

Answer: Because you're asking this question *before* reading the material, *you don't yet have enough information to answer the question.* Don't try to answer it yet. Simply let your mind think about the question while reading the content.

Using Question Words

Some questions deal with large issues and usually require more that one sentence to answer. For example, "**Why** did scientists want to harness nuclear energy?" *Other questions deal with details and may require only a word or two to answer.* For example, "**When** was radioactivity discovered?"

Question Words: How, When, Where, Why, What, Which, Who

Main Idea Question Words: How, Why, What

Example: **Why** did the American colonies decide to declare their independence from England?

Detail Question Words: When, Where, Which, Who, and, sometimes, What (What can be a detail or main idea question word?)

Example: Who discovered radioactivity?

It's time to practice Step 1. Use one of the **Main Idea Question Words** to change the following titles into questions.

Title: "A New Method of Irrigation"
Question: *What was the new irrigation method?*

Title: "Techniques for Reducing Pollution"
Question: _____?

Title: "Salk Discovers a Vaccine That Prevents Polio"
Question: _____?

Title: "New Conservation Techniques in the Rain Forests"
Question: _____?

Title: "The Dangers of Drug Addiction"
Question: _____?

Title: "Three Different Methods of Taxation"

Question: _____?

Now figure out the title from the question.

Question: What were the causes of the Civil War?

Title: "The Causes of the Civil War"

Question: Why did Napoleon invade Russia?

Title: _____

Question: What are the two houses of Congress?

Title: _____

Question: How does the American court system work?

Title: _____

Question: How do cars pollute the environment?

Title: _____

Question: What did Einstein discover?

Title: _____

As previously stated, you completed Step 1 of the Chewing-Up-Information system in Unit 6 when you were mind-mapping and converted the title of the Hundred Years' War unit into a main idea question. If you recall, you wrote, "*What* was the Hundred Years' War" or "*Why* was there a Hundred Years' War?" It is now time to learn three additional steps in the system.

Step 2: Turn each subtitle into a main idea question *before* reading the section. (Use an appropriate main idea question word.)

Reason: This step helps you think about the content of the material you're about to read *before* actually scanning and reading it. The procedure will improve your comprehension.

Subtitle: Social Conditions in the Middle Ages

Question: What were the social conditions in the Middle Ages? (Don't attempt to answer this question yet. Let your mind think about it as you scan.)

Now, go through the unit and turn each subtitle into a Main Idea Question.

Subtitle 1: *Social Conditions in the Middle Ages*

Question 1: What were the social conditions in the Middle Ages?

Subtitle 2: _____

Question 2: _____

Subtitle 3: _____

Question 3: _____

Subtitle 4: _____

Question 4: _____

Subtitle 5: _____

Question 5: _____

Even though you've already done the next step, it's important to do it again because you haven't read the unit for a while.

Step 3: Speed-read the material one time.

The next step is new:

Step 4: Reread the material carefully and use a highlighter or pencil to underline key ideas in each paragraph. (Highlight or underline only the *key words that deal with the important information.*)

Important!

When using the Chewing-Up-Information system, do not underline or highlight your textbook! Other students must use these books next year, and marking in them would not be fair. Later, you'll learn how to take notes and record important information on paper without having to first highlight or underline.

Let's look at how the first five paragraphs might look after you underline or highlight the key ideas (Step 4).

THE HUNDRED YEARS' WAR

Imagine a war between two countries that lasts for more than one hundred years. Then imagine a war in which you, your father, you grandfather, your great grandfather, your great, great grandfather, and your great, great, great grandfather all have fought. This would mean six generations of your family fighting in the same war against the same enemy. Wouldn't that be astounding? Well, such a <u>war</u> actually happened during the <u>Middle Ages.</u> It was <u>called</u> the <u>Hundred Years' War.</u>

The <u>war</u> between <u>France</u> and <u>England</u> <u>began</u> in <u>1337</u> and <u>ended in 1453.</u> During the 116 years that this seemingly never-ending conflict lasted, a succession of <u>five English and five French kings fought</u> for <u>control</u> of <u>France.</u> Because <u>occasional truces</u> and <u>treaties</u> temporarily <u>interrupted</u> the <u>fighting,</u> the <u>war</u> was really a <u>series</u> of <u>wars.</u> The <u>truces,</u> however, were repeatedly <u>broken</u> and the <u>treaties</u> repeatedly <u>discarded</u>; thus two of the most powerful countries in Europe remained locked in an ongoing battle for more than a century.

Social Conditions in the Middle Ages

The <u>Middle Ages</u> (or <u>medieval times</u>) lasted from <u>A.D. 500 to 1500.</u> During this period, there was <u>great social turmoil. By</u> the <u>1300s, feudalism</u>—a system in which great <u>hereditary landowners owned</u> the <u>land</u> and <u>demanded payment</u> and <u>absolute loyalty from peasants</u> working on it—had begun to <u>break down.</u> The <u>power structure shifted,</u> and the <u>feudal lords lost much</u> of their <u>authority.</u> This <u>transformation</u> significantly <u>altered</u> the <u>fabric</u> of <u>medieval society.</u>

<u>While</u> these <u>changes</u> were <u>occurring,</u> the <u>economies</u> of <u>Europe</u> were <u>recovering</u> from a <u>period</u> of <u>decreasing population, social discontent,</u> and <u>shrinking industry</u> and <u>trade. Enriched</u> by this <u>economic improvement,</u> the <u>kings hired armies</u> to <u>enforce their power over</u> the <u>lords.</u> Their <u>well-equipped infantry using new battle strategies</u> and <u>tactics outmatched</u> the <u>weaker armies</u> of the <u>feudal knights</u> and <u>repeatedly defeated them.</u>

The <u>Hundred Years' War interrupted</u> the <u>economic recovery.</u> The <u>continuous conflict</u> between <u>France and England damaged trade</u> and <u>weakened</u> the <u>economies</u> of <u>both countries.</u> At the same time, the <u>Hundred Years' War hastened</u> the <u>breakdown</u> of <u>feudalism</u> and <u>fueled</u> the <u>civil wars</u> that were <u>spreading throughout Europe. Peasants</u> rose in <u>bloody revolts against</u> the <u>lords. Workers in towns clashed</u> with the <u>merchants who denied</u> them a <u>decent wage</u> and <u>kept</u> them <u>powerless.</u>

Underlining or Highlighting on Your Own

Now turn back to the Hundred Years' War unit, and on your own underline or highlight the **key information** in the first five paragraphs. If you have any questions about what is important, refer to the model. When you're finished, compare what you've underlined or highlighted with the model. Your highlighting does not have to be *exactly the same,* but you should make certain that you've underscored all of the key facts. If you discover that you've left information out, consider why this information is important. Do the same with information you highlighted that was not particularly important. This information might be referred to as "fluff." It may be interesting to read, but it's not information that you must recall when studying for a test.

Now carefully reread the rest of the unit and underline or highlight the **key information.** Remember to leave out words such as "a," "the," "their," and "of." Highlight only the important words.

Answering Subtitle Questions

Now that you've completed highlighting, it's time to answer the subtitle questions you posed in **Step 2.** You can refer back to the unit and the information you highlighted to help you answer the questions. Writing the answers to these questions and summarizing what you have studied will help you remember the important information. It will also help you prepare for tests, and it will be especially beneficial if your teachers include essay questions on their tests.

The first two questions are answered for you in the following paragraphs. Answer the third subtitle question on your own.

Step 5: Answer Subtitle Questions and Title Question.

Subtitle Question 1: What were the social conditions in the Middle Ages?

Sample Answer: The Middle Ages lasted from A.D. 500 to 1500, and there was great social turmoil during this period. Feudalism had begun to fail by the 1300s, and the feudal lords, who were hereditary landowners and who demanded money and loyalty from the peasants, began to lose their authority. This resulted in major changes in society. At the same time, the economies of Europe were recovering from decreasing population, social discontent, and reduced trade and production. The kings became rich and hired armies to control the knights. These armies used better battle tactics and defeated the weaker armies of the lords. The Hundred Years' War hurt the economic recovery and weakened trade. It hastened the breakdown of feudalism and fueled civil wars in which the peasants revolted against the lords and workers revolted against the merchants.

Subtitle Question 2: What was the Black Death?

Sample Answer: The bubonic plague was a deadly epidemic spread to humans by fleas that infested infected rats. The epidemic was called the Black Death because of the black spots of dried blood that could be seen under the skin of its victims. Unhygienic conditions produced the ideal environment for the plague to spread. Twenty-five percent of the population of Europe was destroyed between 1347 and 1352.

Subtitle Question 3: What was the role of the Church?

Your Answer: _____

_____

_____

_____

_____

_____

Subtitle Question 4: _____?

Your Answer: _____

_____

_____

_____

_____

_____

Subtitle Question 5: _____?

Your Answer: _____

_____

_____

_____

_____

_____

_____

Title Question: What was the Hundred Years' War?

You've already answered this question in Unit 6. You don't have to answer it again! Now that you've studied the content a second time using a different study method, you may want to add information to your answer to the main idea question. You may want to rewrite your answer, or your teacher may require that you do so. This rewrite will provide an opportunity to hone your summarization and essay-writing skills, and it will allow you to review all of the key information in the unit.

You've now completed the *mind-mapping* and Chewing-Up-Information procedures, and you've undoubtedly learned a great deal about the Hundred Years' War. It's time to take a practice quiz to see just how much you know. Put away your books and your mind-map.

Quiz on the Hundred Years' War

1. The Hundred Years' War
   A. was one continuous battle.
   B. began in 1453 and lasted until 1552.
   C. involved six French kings and six English kings who fought for control of France.
   D. was a series of battles that were temporarily interrupted by truces and treaties.

2. The Middle Ages lasted from A.D. 500 until 1500. **True or False**

3. Feudalism was a system in which the peasants worked on land owned by the king. **True or False**

4. During the 1300s, the power of feudal lords increased, and the power of the king decreased. **True or False**

5. The Hundred Years' War limited the upsurge in the civil wars that were spreading throughout Europe. **True or False**

6. The Hundred Years' War ended the economic recovery that was occurring in Europe. **True or False**

7. The term "Black Death" was used to describe which specific epidemic?

   _____

8. What percentage of the population of Europe died as a result of this epidemic?
   A. 10%
   B. 15%
   C. 25%
   D. 50%

9. The Catholic popes resided in Avignon, France, between
   A. 1203 and 1303.
   B. 1309 and 1377.
   C. 500 and 1500.
   D. 1337 and 1452.

10. The period of turmoil within the Catholic Church when more than one prelate claimed to be pope was called _____

11. The English king whose claim to the French throne in 1337 led to the Hundred Years' War was
    A. Charles IV.
    B. Philip IV.
    C. Edward III.
    D. Philip VI.

12. The first major battle of the Hundred Years' was fought in Crécy, France in _____.

13. The French army was victorious in many of the battles because of the skills of its infantry and its archers, who used rapid-firing long bows. **True or False**

14. The Battle of Crécy was a victory for France under King Philip VI. **True or False**

15. Who led the English army to victory during the second major battle (the Battle of Poitiers in 1356)? _____.

16. The Battle of _____ in 1415 during the reign of Henry V of England was the third major English victory for the Hundred Years' War.

17. In 1420, a treaty called the _____ declared Henry V of England regent of France.

18. The person who led the French army to victory in the Battle of Orleans in 1429 was _____.

19. When the war ended in 1453, England controlled all of Normandy in France. **True or False**

20. After the Hundred Years' War, the nobility and centralized governments in both France and England were weakened. **True or False**

Turn to the last page of this unit to find the answers to this quiz.

EXAMINING YOUR PERFORMANCE ON THE QUIZ

As you have undoubtedly discovered, there were a great number of details that you needed to know to do well on the quiz. Many of the questions were also tricky. Teachers often ask tricky questions to determine whether you've learned and understood the facts that they consider important.

To get a good grade on a test that focuses on facts and details, you must either have strong visual memory skills or you must make a deliberate effort to memorize the information that you read in your textbooks and your notes. If you don't have strong "natural" visual memory skills, don't be discouraged. You'll learn powerful techniques for developing better memory skills in the next unit.

Let's take a look at how you did on the quiz. By giving yourself five points for every correct answer, you can figure out your grade.

Possibility 1: You did very well on the test and received a grade of 90% to 100%. (No more than two incorrect answers.)

Possibility 2: You did well on the test and received a grade of 80% to 85%. (No more than four incorrect answers.)

Possibility 3: You did passably well on the test and received a grade of 70% to 75%. (No more than six incorrect answers.)

Possibility 4: You had difficulty with the test. (Seven or more incorrect answers.)

If you had several incorrect answers, review the information you highlighted. Ask yourself two important questions:

- Did I identify and highlight the information that was covered on the test?
- Did I have difficulty remembering important facts or understanding concepts?

If you had difficulty with the test, don't worry. In Unit 8, you'll learn additional test preparation techniques. You'll also learn how to take "standard notes," and you'll practice answering title and subtitle questions. Because you've already highlighted or underlined the unit, *you've actually done much of the work involved in taking notes.* You'll discover that note taking is easy! All you have to do is transfer this information to your binder.

REVIEWING THE CHEWING-UP-INFORMATION SYSTEM

Number in proper order the five steps that you've learned so far in the **Chewing-Up-Information** system.

Step _____ = Turn each subtitle into a question.

Step _____ = Reread material carefully and highlight or underline key information.

Step _____ = Turn the title into a question using a main idea question word.

Step _____ = Speed-read the material.

Step _____ = Answer subtitle questions and title question.

The **Main Idea Questions** are: _____ _____ _____

The **Detail Questions** are: _____ _____ _____

Questions About Studying

The Chewing-Up-Information system requires too much time, and the potential rewards don't justify spending this much time.	T	F
You should always use a highlighter in your textbooks.	T	F
Mind-mapping is fun, but it's more like a game and isn't very useful.	T	F
Mind-mapping helps you link, understand, and remember what you study.	T	F
Before mind-mapping, you should speed read the material.	T	F
As long as you memorize the important information when you study, you're guaranteed to get good grades on tests.	T	F
Taking the time to ask and answer questions when you study and writing short essay answers can improve your comprehension and recall.	T	F
You should pose main idea and subtitle questions before carefully reading the content.	T	F
You should answer the questions about the title and subtitles before reading the content.	T	F
When you make a mistake, figuring out what went wrong reduces the chances of repeating the same mistake.	T	F
When taking textbook notes, you should try to write down as much as you can.	T	F
Reading material one or two times is sufficient when studying for a test.	T	F

Unit 8

Taking and Using Textbook Notes

For Teachers

Objectives

This unit teaches students how to take textbook notes in traditional standard form. Students also learn how to write powerful, effective, and cogent short essays that demonstrate their understanding and retention of key information, and they learn how to distinguish main ideas from details when using their notes to study.

LESSON PLAN

1. In **Getting the Job Done,** students examine the study strategy of a highly goal-directed student.

2. In **Evaluating Carlos's Plan and Making Predictions,** students evaluate the protagonist's modus operandi and predict the consequences of his study plan.

3. In **Learning How to Take Notes**, students review the first five steps of the **"Chewing-Up Information"** system. They use the information they've already highlighted in the Hundred Years' War unit and convert it into standard notes.

4. In **Practicing Taking Notes,** students continue taking notes on the entire Hundred Years' War unit.

5. In **Using Abbreviations,** students review common abbreviations that they can use to take notes more rapidly

6. In **More Practice Taking Notes,** students apply the **Chewing-Up-Information** system to a facsimile science unit about global warming. They examine sample notes[1] covering the first section of the unit and then practice taking notes on the entire unit without first highlighting or underlining. They compare their notes with the model and examine the similarities and differences between their notes and the sample.

7. In **Learning How to Answer Essay Questions,** students examine and discuss the modeled topic and concluding sentences. They should use these models as guidelines while writing their answers to the *subtitle (main idea) questions* **(Step 5)** that they posed before they taking notes.

8. Before beginning **Answering the Title Question (Step 6),** students practice writing a "thumbnail outline." After completing their essays, they compare them with the model essays.

9. In **Distinguishing Main Ideas From Details**, students learn how to use their notes to study and review for tests. They use highlighters to color-code information in their notes and to distinguish main ideas from facts and details **(Step 7).**

10. In **Review of How to Take and Use Textbook Notes** and **Review of How to Use Essay Questions as a Study Tool,** students complete checklists to reinforce the procedures they've learned.

IDENTIFYING AND RECORDING IMPORTANT INFORMATION

Most underperforming high school students have a marginal understanding about how to identify, assimilate, and retain important information when they read and study. If asked how they would prepare for a test, their typical response would probably be, "I guess I'd reread the chapter and look at my notes." Of course, defeated learners who are resigned to failure might not even bother to study at all.

An analysis of the study procedures of struggling students usually indicates that they don't have a clue about learning actively. In most instances, their poor grades are a direct function of deficient reading comprehension skills, passive

---

1. The sample notes can be used in reproducible format and/or can also be reproduced on a transparency and projected onto a screen. Projecting the notes onto a screen could facilitate a class discussion.

learning, inadequate study habits, poor recall, and an inability to anticipate what their teachers are likely to consider important and the questions their teachers are likely to ask on tests.

Being able to take good textbook notes is a critically important component in an effective test preparation methodology. Unfortunately, most underachieving students have never adequately mastered this fundamental study procedure. These students typically take notes mechanically and without engaging themselves actively in the process.

Teachers often assume that students entering high school know how to take notes and how to study for tests. In many cases, this is wishful thinking. Relatively few school districts mandate that study skills be systematically taught in elementary or middle school. Whereas "natural" students can usually figure out how to take effective notes without formal training, the vast majority of teenagers in the typical classroom are *not* natural students. These students require methodical note-taking instruction, repeated opportunities to practice, and incisive feedback.

Successful students realize their notes can help them understand and recall what they're studying. They also realize that the note-taking procedure helps them extract, distill, and link key information in their textbook and lectures. Although they know taking notes initially requires extra time, they also recognize that note taking can play an instrumental role in their getting better grades and could actually reduce their total study time. Instead of having to reread and extract key information from an assigned textbook unit when preparing for a test, they can expedite their study time by reviewing their notes. All the important information that they need to study productively should be right there.

Intellectually passive learners have a very different operating routine. These students are likely to take the path of least resistance and avoid any steps that might involve additional effort. Taking detailed textbook notes would certainly qualify as a course of action that passive learners would be predisposed to shun. If these students are to improve their study procedures, they must be guided to key insights: (1) taking textbook notes is a powerful study tool and (2) the process becomes easier and less time-consuming with practice.

Some teachers believe that it's not only acceptable but actually desirable to teach note taking by having students copy the teacher's own notes from the chalkboard. The typical justification for this mind-dulling practice is that the copied notes provide a standardized model and ensure uniformity and quality. What these teachers may fail to recognize is that copying notes from the chalkboard encourages passive learning. In effect, the teacher is doing all of the thinking.

In contrast, teaching students how to identify and record what's important in their content area courses and teaching them how to take notes on their own stimulates active learning. The process of methodically extracting information forces students to think about what they're reading, identify what's important, and make judgments about the relative value of specific data. This active learning can't help but enhance comprehension, assimilation, and retention.

SUMMARY OF STUDENT EXERCISES AND ACTIVITIES

Examining the Story

Students read the case study and evaluate the protagonist's study strategy and diligence. They then predict the effects of his strategy.

Learning How to Take Textbook Notes and Practicing Taking Notes

The procedure of underlining or highlighting key data in textbooks is intended to serve as a precursor to learning how to take traditional notes. In this exercise, students review the first five steps of the Chewing-Up-Information system that were introduced in the Unit 7. They discover that the information they previously targeted can be easily transferred into a standard note-taking format. After studying the provided modeled notes, students then transfer the information they've already highlighted into standard notes, and they continue to take notes on the entire Hundred Years' War unit. Students should be reminded that they're in the process of learning a new study method and that highlighting is permitted only on the reproducible sheets and not in their textbooks. Once they learn how to identify important information, they'll begin taking notes without having to highlight or underline school-owned textbooks.

More Practice Taking Notes

This exercise reinforces the note-taking skills introduced in the previous exercise. Students use the Chewing-Up-Information system and note taking to study systematically a facsimile science unit about global warming. They speed-read the unit and turn the title and subtitles into main idea questions. They then take notes on the unit.

Completed Model Notes

Students examine model notes from the global warming unit. They compare their own notes to the sample notes and discuss why certain material was or was not included. To reinforce mastery, students should practice and reinforce the note-taking procedure using one of their textbooks. This may be assigned as either an in-class or homework project.

Learning How to Answer Essay Questions

Students examine and discuss model topic and concluding sentences. They then use their notes to answer the subtitle questions about the global warming unit. The goal is for students to have additional practice summarizing the important information they recorded in their notes and to improve their expository writing skills.

Model Essays

Once students have completed their essays, they compare them with the model essays that are provided. A class discussion should focus on any problems that they may have encountered.

Students' essays obviously do not have to be the same as the models. The modeled essays are intended to represent a standard toward which they can aim. The objective is for students to realize that first-rate language arts skills, like athletic skills, develop with effort, practice, and feedback from a teacher (or coach). You should emphasize the specific elements that distinguish an effective essay from an ineffective essay, namely:

1. Good topic sentences

2. Inclusion of important and relevant information

3. Organized and logical presentation of ideas

4. Correct grammar

5. Varied sentence structure

6. Correct punctuation

7. Correct spelling

8. Good concluding sentences

9. Conclusions that can be justified by the information contained in the essay

Answering the Title Question

Students learn how to make a quick "thumbnail" outline of key information they want to include in their overview essay. They use this information to write a concise but inclusive short essay that answers the title question that they posed before they began taking notes. They then compare their essay with the model provided. During a class discussion, students examine and discuss the content of their own essays and compare them with the model. To avoid embarrassing students whose language arts skills are weak, participation in this class discussion and the sharing of essays with classmates should be voluntary.

Distinguishing Main Ideas From Details

Students carefully review their notes and use highlighters, felt markers, or colored pencils to differentiate and color-code the main ideas and details. (This is Step 7 of the Chewing-Up-Information system.) You want students to realize that this differentiation procedure is an effective final review technique when studying for tests. Urge students to anticipate whether the teachers of their content area subjects are likely to ask detail questions or main idea (essay) questions on a test. During a class discussion, examine the reasons some teachers prefer to use multiple-choice, true–false, or short-answer questions when designing tests, and other teachers prefer essay questions. (Many teachers, of course, use a combination of different types of questions on their tests.)

Encourage students to review their previous tests when they study and to identify the kinds of questions their teachers typically ask. Also urge them to consider the type of information they're studying. Certain information (e.g., facts and details) lends itself to multiple-choice tests, true–false, short-answer, and fill-in-the-blanks questions, whereas other information (e.g., concepts) lends itself to essay exams. Students who study strategically factor this into their study plan when preparing for tests.

In the final activity, students complete two checklists that review and reinforce the study skills they've learned. These checklists can be an ideal catalyst for a dynamic class discussion.

Unit 8

Taking and Using Textbook Notes

For Students

GETTING THE JOB DONE

For as long as he could remember, Carlos wanted to be an attorney. As his parents and friends repeatedly reminded him, he loved to argue. Even when he was only five years old, his parents and relatives were already telling him that he would make a great lawyer.

Carlos enjoyed any movie or TV program about lawyers. The idea of defending someone in court intrigued him. It was like being an actor on stage. Only in the case of a *real* criminal attorney, you weren't playing a part in a movie, and you weren't pretending. The defendant's fate would be in his hands, and his skills could determine whether this person went to prison or was acquitted. For Carlos, nothing could conceivably be more exciting than representing an innocent person and winning an acquittal.

Realizing he would have to go to college and law school, Carlos was determined to get good grades. His family didn't have a lot of money, and he knew he would need a scholarship. He also knew he wouldn't have a chance of earning a scholarship to a first-rate university unless he had an excellent GPA and excellent letters of recommendation from his teachers.

Carlos's immediate goal was to get an A on the biology chapter test he would be taking the following Monday. The test might make the difference between him getting a B+ or an A– in the course. Although biology wasn't one of his favorite subjects, getting the A– was extremely important to Carlos given his long-range goals.

Carlos had seven days to prepare for the test. Aware that he needed to develop an effective study strategy, he devised the following:

Study Plan

Monday	Speed-read assigned biology chapter twice.
	Make up main idea and detail questions from title and subtitles.
	Read the chapter carefully.
	Mind-map the chapter.
Tuesday	Reread chapter carefully.
	Expand mind-map to improve comprehension.
Wednesday	Take notes in "standard form."
	Answer questions from title and subtitles.
	Review class notes and identify details and concepts.
	Write important facts on index cards and memorize the key data.
Thursday	Make up practice test questions from notes based on types of questions teacher has asked on previous biology chapter tests.
Weekend	Review class notes, textbook notes, and mind-map one final time.

Carlos estimated that his plan would require a total of approximately five hours and thirty minutes of study time. If he spent forty-five minutes studying biology every evening and studied two hours and forty-five minutes over the weekend, he could make the plan work. Carlos didn't consider five and a half hours too high a price to pay for a good grade on an important test. An A– in the course would maintain his overall GPA. Carlos felt that his study plan was on target. He liked being on target, and he especially liked achieving his goals.

EXAMINING THE STORY

Based on the description of Carlos's attitude and behavior, evaluate him in the following areas.

How would you evaluate Carlos's study plan?

1	2	3	4	5	6	7	8	9	10
Not Smart			**Fairly Smart**				**Very Smart**		

How would you evaluate Carlos's diligence and effort?

1	2	3	4	5	6	7	8	9	10
Not Smart			**Fairly Smart**				**Very Smart**		

How would you evaluate Carlos's strategic thinking skills?

1	2	3	4	5	6	7	8	9	10
Not Smart			**Fairly Smart**				**Very Smart**		

Based on the description of Carlos's attitude and behavior, make the following predictions.

If Carlos follows his plan, how would you rate his chances of getting an A– on the biology test?

1	2	3	4	5	6	7	8	9	10
Not Likely			**Fairly Likely**				**Very Likely**		

Do you think that Carlos will follow his study plan?

1	2	3	4	5	6	7	8	9	10
Not Likely			**Fairly Likely**				**Very Likely**		

How would you rate Carlos's chances being accepted at a good college?

1	2	3	4	5	6	7	8	9	10
Not Likely			**Fairly Likely**				**Very Likely**		

How would you rate Carlos's chances earning a scholarship?

1	2	3	4	5	6	7	8	9	10
Not Likely			**Fairly Likely**				**Very Likely**		

How would you rate Carlos's chances of going to law school and becoming a lawyer?

1	2	3	4	5	6	7	8	9	10
Not Likely			**Fairly Likely**				**Very Likely**		

How would you rate Carlos's chances of becoming a good lawyer?

1	2	3	4	5	6	7	8	9	10
Not Likely			**Fairly Likely**				**Very Likely**		

Why did you make the preceding predictions?

_____

_____

_____

LEARNING HOW TO TAKE NOTES

You've already learned and used many powerful study tools and techniques. These include:

- Asking questions when you study
- Mind-mapping
- Chewing-up-information
- Identifying important information
- Distinguishing main ideas from details

In Unit 7, you learned and practiced the **"Chewing-Up-Information"** **system.** In Step 4 of this procedure, you highlighted or underlined important information, and you were cautioned that because you aren't allowed to underline or highlight in your regular textbooks, this highlighting step was for practice only.

It's now time to learn another way to organize and record information without having to highlight your textbooks. The method is called **standard note taking.** _The first three steps of this note-taking method are the same as in the Chewing-Up-Information_ system, but instead of highlighting or underlining important information, you transfer this information directly into notes.

Let's review the four steps of the Chewing-Up-Information system:

Step 1. Turn the title into a question _before_ reading the material. (Main idea question words: _How, Why, What._)

Write the title question on the top line of your notebook paper and begin writing at the margin.

Step 2. Turn each subtitle into a question before reading the material.

Indent below the title question and leave plenty of space to put your notes under each question. Use a pencil or erasable pen in case you want to make changes.

Step 3. Speed-read the material.

Step 4. Read the material carefully and write down key information in note form as you read.

Do not highlight. Instead, begin taking notes. (A sample of standard note taking is found on pages 163–164.)

You're now going to put the key information you underlined in the Hundred Years' War unit into **standard note-taking form.** Remember:

- Write down only key information
- Leave out unnecessary words

- Abbreviate whenever possible
- Write neatly and legibly
- Indent your notes under each question

When taking notes under each subtitle question, don't try to answer the question in your notes. Write down only the key information that deals with the section. When you finish taking notes, you'll use your notes to answer each subtitle question (Step 5).

USING ABBREVIATIONS

Although you can save time using abbreviations when you take notes, it's essential that you be able to understand your own abbreviations! Following are some abbreviations you may want to use. These abbreviations are different from the assignment-recording abbreviations that were presented in Unit 3. Feel free to make up your own abbreviation, but make sure that you understand them!

Abbreviations for Note Taking

" = inch	comp = complete	info = information	th = the
' = foot	diff = difficult	mid = middle	thru = through
< = less than	dur = during	min = minute	tm = time
> = more than	dy = day	mny = many	u = you
2 = to	Eng = English	mo = month	un = unit
2gthr = together	ex = example	n/t = next to	v = very
→ = thus	exer = exercise	nt = not	w = with
abv = above	fn = finish	nxt = next	w/o = without
Amer = American	fr = for	p = page	wch = which
bg = big	Fr = French	per = person	wdth = width
bio = biology	frm = from	ques = question	wh = what
blw = below	gd = good	sec = second	wh = who
bot = bottom	his = history	sect = section	wn = when
cen = century	hr = hour	sm = small	whr = where
ch = chapter	ht = height	Sp = Spanish	y = why
chem = chemistry	imp = important	t/o = throughout	yr = year

Personalized abbreviations:

____ = _____   ____ = _____   ____ = _____   ____ = _____
____ = _____   ____ = _____   ____ = _____   ____ = _____

Many words can be abbreviated and clearly understood simply by leaving out vowels. For example: pls = please; mny = many; words = wrds; understood = undrstd; vowels = vwls.

PRACTICING TAKING NOTES

In Unit 7, you highlighted or underlined the important information found in the first five paragraphs of Hundred Years' War unit. You're now going to transfer this information into standard notes. The first part of the unit and the underlined key information are reproduced here. Model notes for this section can be found on pages 165–167.

THE HUNDRED YEARS' WAR

Imagine a war between two countries that lasts for more than one hundred years. Then imagine a war in which you, your father, you grandfather, your great grandfather, your great, great grandfather, and your great, great, great grandfather all have fought. This would mean six generations of your family fighting in the same war against the same enemy. Wouldn't that be astounding? Well, such a <u>war</u> actually happened during the <u>Middle Ages.</u> It was <u>called</u> the <u>Hundred Years' War.</u>

The war between <u>France</u> and <u>England</u> <u>began</u> in <u>1337</u> and <u>ended in 1453.</u> During the 116 years that this seemingly never-ending conflict lasted, a succession of <u>five English and five French kings fought</u> for <u>control</u> of <u>France.</u> Because <u>occasional truces</u> and <u>treaties</u> temporarily <u>interrupted</u> the <u>fighting,</u> the <u>war</u> was really a <u>series</u> of <u>wars.</u> The <u>truces,</u> however, were repeatedly <u>broken</u> and the <u>treaties</u> were repeatedly <u>discarded;</u> thus two of the most powerful countries in Europe remained locked in an ongoing battle for more than a century.

Social Conditions in the Middle Ages

The <u>Middle Ages</u> (or <u>medieval times</u>) lasted from A.D. <u>500</u> to <u>1500</u>. During this period, there was <u>great social turmoil.</u> <u>By</u> the <u>1300s,</u> <u>feudalism</u>—a system in which great <u>hereditary landowners owned</u> the <u>land</u> and <u>demanded payment</u> and <u>absolute loyalty</u> <u>from peasants</u> working on it—had begun to <u>break down.</u> The <u>power structure shifted,</u> and the <u>feudal lords lost much</u> of their <u>authority.</u> This <u>transformation</u> significantly <u>altered</u> the <u>fabric</u> of <u>medieval society.</u>

While these <u>changes</u> were <u>occurring,</u> the <u>economies</u> of <u>Europe</u> were <u>recovering</u> from a <u>period</u> of <u>decreasing population, social discontent,</u> and <u>shrinking industry</u> and <u>trade.</u> <u>Enriched</u> by this <u>economic improvement,</u> the <u>kings hired armies</u> to <u>enforce their power over</u> the <u>lords.</u> Their <u>well-equipped infantry using new battle strategies</u> and <u>tactics</u> <u>outmatched</u> the <u>weaker armies</u> of the <u>feudal knights</u> and <u>repeatedly defeated them.</u>

The <u>Hundred Years' War interrupted</u> the <u>economic recovery.</u> The <u>continuous conflict</u> between <u>France and England</u> <u>damaged trade</u> and <u>weakened</u> the <u>economies</u> of <u>both countries.</u> At the same time, the <u>Hundred Years' War</u> <u>hastened</u> the <u>breakdown</u> of <u>feudalism</u> and <u>fueled</u> the <u>civil wars</u> that were <u>spreading throughout Europe.</u> <u>Peasants</u> rose in <u>bloody revolts against</u> the <u>lords.</u> <u>Workers in towns clashed</u> with the <u>merchants who denied</u> them a <u>decent wage</u> and <u>kept</u> them <u>powerless.</u>

NOTES

(Main idea title question)

What was the Hundred Years' War?

Dring Middle Ages →wr Frnce/Englnd → 1337–1453

5 Eng./5 Fr. Kings fought cntrl Frnce.

Occas. Truces/treaties → series wrs

Truces brokn/treaties discrdd

Main idea subtitle question: What Were the Social Conditions in Middle Ages?

Middle Age (medieval times) A.D. 500–1500 → great soc. trmoil

By 1300s feudlsm—herditry lndownrs ownd lnd—dmnded payment & abslute loylty frm peasnt→pwer struc. Shft→feudal lords lst authorty→ chnged soc.

Eur. econ. recovrng dcreasng popul→ soc. discontnt, shrnkng indstry & trde.

Rch kngs hired armies enfrce pwr over lrds

Well-eqped infntry used nw bttle strateg & tactcs dfeat knghts.

100 years wr interrup. econ rcvcry→damgd trade & econ. of both cntries.

Wr hastned breakdwn feudal, fueld civ. wrs sprdng t/o Eur. →psnts bldy rvolts agnst lrds→ wrkrs twns clshed mechnts about wges & pwr

Copy the preceding notes onto binder paper. Refer back to Hundred Years' War unit (pages 117–120) in Unit 7. Complete highlighting or underlining the important information in the entire unit and then transfer the key information into standard note-taking form. Take notes on the entire unit. *Remember: Begin by turning each subtitle into a question and then record the important relevant information.*

MORE PRACTICE TAKING NOTES

You're now going to use the Chewing-Up-Information system to study the following science unit. This time, however, you will proceed to taking notes *without underlining or highlighting first.* Before you begin to take notes, review the sample notes on pages 163–164.

Remember: Don't highlight or underline. After completing Steps 1–3, start taking notes.

Notes on the first section of the global warming unit are modeled on pages 160–164. Copy these notes onto your binder paper and continue taking notes on the rest of the unit. Write neatly and indent when recording key information. This will help when you study for tests. Your notes should resemble the sample notes on pages 163–164.

GLOBAL WARMING:
THE EARTH ON A HOTPLATE

Earth's surface temperature has fluctuated during the millions of years since the planet was formed. At one time, great sheets of glacial ice covered large portions of the world's landmass. Later, periods of warmer temperature forced the glaciers to retreat. In view of these periodic fluctuations, should we be legitimately concerned when we discover that the average temperature on the surface of the earth has increased by .5 to 1.5 degrees Fahrenheit (.3 to .8 degrees Celsius) during the last one hundred years? Is an increase of only one degree all that important?

Scientists and government policy makers throughout the world are currently debating the issue of global warming. Some find the temperature increase to be temporary and insignificant. Others are far more alarmed by what they perceive to be a major threat to the word's ecology. Based on current trends, these concerned scientists believe that the earth's surface temperature might rise from 3 to 8 degrees Fahrenheit (1.5 to 4.5 degrees Celsius) by the year 2100. They also point out that during the last thirty years, the average surface air temperature has actually increased more rapidly than at any time in recorded history.

Despite disagreements about the causes and potential impact of global warming, most scientists acknowledge that an additional increase of three to five degrees could have a major, and perhaps even catastrophic, impact on the world's ecosystems (the interaction of living organisms and physical environment within a region). Such an increase could make the world that we know a very different place.

The Impact of Human Behavior on Climate

Many scientists are convinced that human beings are primarily responsible for the current global warming trend. They contend that the extensive burning of carbon-based fossil fuels such as coal, oil, and natural gas to power the internal combustion engines in motor vehicles, generate electricity, heat and air-condition buildings, and run factories has boosted the amounts of carbon dioxide and other gases emitted into the atmosphere. The widespread burning of wood to generate heat also boosts the amount of atmospheric carbon and gases.

Approximately 6 billion tons of carbon are emitted into the atmosphere each year as a result of the combustion of fossil fuels. It is estimated that 176 billion tons of carbon were emitted between 1850 and 1980.

The monitoring of atmospheric levels of carbon dioxide (CO_2), a primary by-product when fossil fuels burn, began in 1958. Monitoring devices positioned at an altitude of 11,000 feet above sea level in Hawaii indicate a steady increase in atmospheric carbon dioxide. Comparisons of current atmospheric CO_2 levels with those in air trapped in ice bubbles in 1880 indicate that the CO_2 levels are now 25 percent higher.

Scientists alarmed by the massive release of carbon into the atmosphere believe that CO_2 could be slowing the rate at which heat escapes from the earth.

These scientists contend that the retention of heat in the atmosphere could be causing the temperature on the earth's surface to rise and that this phenomenon is accelerating global warming.

The extensive deforestation of tropical and conifer (cone-bearing trees and plants) forests for lumber and fuel and to make way for farms, highways, towns, and cities adds to the problem of global warming. Vast areas of land that were once covered with trees and plants have been transformed into shopping malls and ever-expanding urban communities. The construction of homes, factories, and businesses are continually encroaching on the vegetation that breaks down carbon dioxide and regenerates the earth's supply of oxygen through the process of photosynthesis. Lush rain forests have been harvested for wood products, and many have been destroyed. This deforestation has not only had a negative impact on the societies of native peoples living in these rain forests, it has caused species of plant and animal life living in these habitats to become extinct or seriously threatened. In fact, a recent analysis published in the journal *Nature*, conducted by scientists using climate forecasts and computer models in fourteen laboratories throughout the world, concluded that more than one-third of the 1,103 native species that they studied could vanish or become nearly extinct by 2050.

Scientists who believe that modern-day energy usage practices have increased the atmospheric gases that trap heat warn that the warming phenomenon could alter rainfall patterns and have a disastrous impact on the earth's ecosystems. Habitats may be radically transformed, and species that are unable to adjust to these changes are at risk for becoming extinct. The increase in the earth's surface temperature could melt polar ice, raise sea levels, and cause coastal areas to become inundated. Beaches would disappear, and low-lying areas and seacoast towns and cities would be flooded. Deltas along the Nile River in Egypt, the Ganges River in India, and the Mississippi River in the United States could be transformed into swamps. Fishing-based cultures would be destroyed. Ports could become inoperable, and this could have a devastating impact on maritime commerce. Global warming could also increase the frequency and severity of tropical storms and alter existing weather patterns that, in turn, could jeopardize food production. Agricultural and cattle grazing areas that are now fertile may become barren and desolate, and some farmlands could become dustbowls or even deserts.

Natural Changes in Climate

The periodic changes in global climate have had a great impact not only on species survival, but also on human society. For example, the climate in northern areas was once milder than today. This made it possible for the Vikings in A.D. 985 to migrate from Iceland to Greenland, which historically has always been colder than Iceland, and establish settlements. Later, when the northern climate became colder again, the Viking decided to abandon these settlements.

In the past, changes in global climate were linked to naturally occurring phenomena. Cloud cover, ocean currents such as El Niño (a periodic warming of the temperature of the Pacific Ocean off the coast of South America), and variations in the amount of radiation produced by the sun have played instrumental roles in altering the earth's surface temperature. Major volcanic eruptions that spew millions of tons of sunlight-blocking ash and gases into the atmosphere have also altered the earth's weather. An example of the impact of these naturally occurring disasters can be found in the 1991 volcanic eruption on Mount Pinatubo on the island of Luzon in the Philippines. The erupting volcano emitted large amounts of sulfur gas and ash into the atmosphere, and this affected weather patterns worldwide. Scientists believe that the massive eruption on Mount Pinatubo resulted in a decrease of 1.1 degrees Fahrenheit (0.6 degrees Celsius) in global temperature that lasted for several years.

The Greenhouse Effect

The greenhouse effect refers to the heat-trapping gases that keep the earth's surface considerably warmer than it might be otherwise. These gases, which include carbon dioxide, methane, and water vapor, were being produced long before human beings appeared on the earth. Animals breathe in oxygen, burn energy, and emit CO_2. By means of photosynthesis, plants and trees break down much of this CO_2 and convert it into oxygen. This recycling of oxygen and carbon dioxide is essential to land-based forms of life.

The greenhouse effect is actually a positive phenomenon that makes the earth habitable to animals and fauna. Each day the sun bathes the earth in radiant energy in the form of light and heat. Some of this radiant energy is reflected by the earth's atmosphere back into space, and some is absorbed by the earth's surface and then radiated back into the atmosphere in the form of heat. Greenhouse gases trap and absorb the heat that warms the atmosphere. Were it not for the greenhouse effect, the earth would be cold and desolate, and life as we know it would not exist.

Of concern is whether human beings and their activities are magnifying the greenhouse effect and jeopardizing the natural cycles and balances. This concern is underscored by the fact that during the last two decades, record high annual global temperatures have been recorded; 1995 was the warmest year on record. At the same time, research indicates that the carbon content in the atmosphere is now higher than at any time during the past 160,000 years.

Preventing Global Warming

The potential harm from global warming has prompted concerned scientists to propose strategies for reducing the quantity of greenhouse gases that are emitted into the atmosphere. One of the key recommendations is to develop new technology that increases energy efficiency, lowers energy usage, reduces the massive amounts of fossil fuels that are being consumed, and lowers the emission and accumulation of greenhouse gases. Practical applications of these recommendations include developing less energy-wasteful electrical motors to run air-conditioners, refrigerators, fans, stoves, and dishwashers; encouraging the use of more energy-efficient light bulbs; and requiring that better insulation be used to retain heat in winter and cold in summer. Although the installation of new energy efficient technology and equipment may be costly initially, the long-range savings in energy consumption could more than offset these costs.

Making automobile engines more energy efficient is another obvious means for reducing fossil-fuel consumption. Cars that run on powerful batteries and electric motors and hybrid motor vehicles that combine small fossil-fuel internal combustion engines with self-recharging electric engines are proving viable alternatives the gas-guzzling models that have been the mainstay of the world automobile industry for decades. This new automotive technology reduces the use of fossil fuels and lessens the greenhouse gases that are emitted into the atmosphere. Engineers are also making considerable headway in developing automobiles that are powered by nonfossil fuels such as hydrogen. These cars emit no heat-trapping gases.

A more controversial strategy for regulating the burning of fossil fuels has also been proposed. The plan would place limits on the total amount of greenhouse gases that each country is permitted to emit into the atmosphere. Countries could buy, sell, or trade their permits. In this way, prosperous developed countries with higher emissions rates could purchase permits from less prosperous developing countries that emit fewer gases. Richer countries would have monetary incentives to lower their greenhouse gas emissions but, at the same time, their economies would not be excessively hampered by the restrictions. Poorer countries would receive funds for selling permits that they don't require and could use the money to accelerate their own economic development.

Despite any controversies about the causes and the seriousness of global warming that might exists, it is clear that the phenomenon requires close monitoring. If the temperature of the earth is indeed rising precipitously and if the actions of human beings are indeed responsible for this trend, there must be intervention. Human beings are remarkably clever and ingenious, and their resourcefulness must be used to address the issue of global warming before irreparable ecological damage occurs. Our planet is resilient and enduring, but at the same time, its ecology is fragile and vulnerable. Our very existence could depend on our deliberately protecting and preserving the vital balances that exist in nature.[2]

Sample Notes

Main idea title question: *What is global warming?*

Introduction

Earth's surfce temp flctuates

---

2. Sources: *World Book* and *Encyclopedia Britannica*.

Grt shts ice once coverd lndmass→temp. rose & glciers retreated

Avrg. Temp incrse 1 dgree last 100 yrs

Scien. and polcy mkers debating glbl wrming→some not cncrned→others alrmed

Cur. Trnds→temp mght rse 3–8 dgrees

Temp incse dring lst 30 yrs mre rapd any tme hstry

Incrse 3–5 dgrs could hve majr impct work ecosystms

Subtitle Question: How does human behavior have an impact on climate?

Mny scntst cnvncd humans rspnsible globl wrmng

Brnng carbn-bsed fossil fuels—coal, old, natur gas—cars, electrcty, heat/air cond./factries→burning of wood→CO_2 relsed into air

6 B tns of crbn emttd each yr atmsphre

176 B tns carbn btwn 1859 and 1980

Monitrng bgn 1958→11000 ft Hawaii.

Compar currnt atmsphr CO_2 air bbles 1880→ CO_2 25% hghr→possbly slwng rte heat escpe frm earth→ heat rtaind atmsphre→temp earth surfc rises→global warming

Defrstation trop and conifer trs and plnts→frms, hghwys, twns, cties→hmes, shppng mlls etc→contrbt glbal wrmng→destry veg that brks dwn CO_2 into O thru photosynthesis→ rain forsts detryd→specs bcmng extnct →impct natve pple

Incrse heat-trppng gses could altr rainfll pttrns & dmge ecosystms→habtts chnged→ species unble adjst→exnct→polr ice mlt→sea levls rse→coatl areas flded→beachs dsppr→lw-lyng areas & cties/twns inndted→deltas Nile, Ganges, Mississ. R. swmps→fshng dstryd→ports inopprable→maritime commrs hurt→weathr pttrns chngd→food produc hurt→aggrcltural & grzing areas dstryd→farmlnds→ dustbowls/deserts

Copy these sample notes on binder paper and then complete taking notes on the entire unit. Use the sample notes as a model. Write neatly. You can make up your own abbreviations, but if you do, *make sure you can understand them later!* Leave out information you don't think is important, but include information your teachers might consider important, even if you don't agree. (This is called "thinking like the teacher," and good students do this all the time!) **IMPORTANT: Don't look at the completed sample notes until**

you've completed your own! You should do your *own thinking* about what to include and what to leave out. If you simply copy the sample notes, you won't learn the thinking process that is linked to effective note taking. After completing your own notes, compare them with the sample and add any important information you may have left out. Your notes do not have to be exactly the same as those in the model. You may also, of course, use fewer or different abbreviations.

COMPLETED MODEL NOTES

Main idea title question: *What is global warming?*

Introduction

Earth's surfce temp has fluctuated

Grt shts ice once coverd lndmass→temp. rose & glciers retreated

Avrg. Temp incrse 1 dgree last 100 yrs

Scien. and polcy mkers debating glbl wrming→some not cncrned→others alrmed

Cur. Trnds→temp mght rse 3–8 dgrees

Temp incse dring lst 30 yrs mre rapd any tme hstry

Incrse 3–5 dgrs could hve majr impct work ecosystms

Subtitle question: *How does human behavior have an impact on climate?*

Mny scntsts cnvncd humans rspnsble glbl wrmng

Brnng carbn-bsed fossil fuels—coal, oil, natur gas—cars, electrcty, heat/air

cond./factries→burning of wood→CO_2 relsed into air

6 B tns of crbn emttd each yr atmsphre

176 B tns carbn btwn 1859 and 1980

Monitrng bgn 1958→11000 ft Hawaii.

Compar currnt atmsphr CO_2 air bbles 1880→ CO_2 25% hghr→possbly slwng rte heat escpe frm earth→heat rtaind atmsphre→temp earth surfc rises→global warming

Defrstation trop and conifer trs and plnts→frms, hghwys, twns, cties→hmes, shppng mlls etc→contrbt glbal wrmng→destry veg brk dwn CO_2 into O→photosynthesis→rain forsts detryd→specs bcmng extnct →impct natve pple→Scntst stdy in 14 cntries: 1/3 of 1103 species stdied could vansh by 2050

Incrse heat-trppng gses could altr rainfll pttrns & dmge ecosystms →habtts chnged→species unble adjst→exnct→polr ice mlt→sea levls rse→coatl areas flded→beachs dsppr→lw-lyng areas & cties/twns inndted→deltas Nile, Ganges, Mississ. R. swmps→fshng dstryd→ports inopprable→maritime commrs hurt→weathr pttrns chngd→food produc hurt→aggrcltural and grzing areas dstryd→farmlnds→dustbowls/ deserts

Subtitle question: *Why are there natural changes in climate?*

Chngs glbl climte impct on spcies srvival & humn socty

Clmte north once mildr thn tday→Vikings A.D. 985 migrted frm Icelnd to

Grnland→becme clder→abandne sttlemnts

Bfr glbl climte chnges linked natur phnmnon→cloud cver, ocn currnts (el Nino), variants amnt sun radiatn, vlcnc errup→spew ash & gses in atmshere→Mt. Pinatubo 1991 Luzon/Phllppns→sufur gs & ash affcttd weathr pttrns wrldwide→decrse 1.1 F. dgrs svral yrs

Subtitle question: *What is the greenhouse effect?*

GHE→heat-trpping gses keep atmsphr wrm→CO_2, methane, wter vpr→ exsted bfr humns

Anmls breath O, brn enrgy, emit CO_2, convrt O via photosynthesis

GH naturl→earth bathd radiant enrgy as lght & heat→sme rflcted by atmsphr bck to spce→sme absrbe erths srfc→radiatd bck into atmsphr as heat→GH gses trp & absrb heat→atmsphr wrmed→w/o gh effct→earth cld & life wouldn't exst

Issue→humns & actvties mgnfyng gh effct & undrmng blances→lst 2 dcdes rcrd hgh glbl temp. 1995 wrmst on recrd→crbn cntnt atmsphr hghest in 160,000 yrs

Subtitle question: *How can global warming be prevented?*

Strtgies for rdcing gh effct→devlp new tech incrse enrgy efficncy, lwer enrgy use, rdce fssil fuels consmmed, lwr emssn & accmltn of gh gases→ bter elec mtrs fr air cndtners, fns, rfrgrtors, stves, dshwshrs, enrgy effic lght blbs, bttr insltion.

New tech mr expnsve intlly→offst svngs on enrgy

Auto engns mre enrgy efficnt→battries/elec mtrs→hybrid internl cmbstion/slf-rechrgng elec engns→redces use fssl fuels, lssns gh gases in atmsphr→auto pwrd by non-fssl fuels ex. Hydrogen→emit no ht-trppng gses.

Contrvrsal pln→limt amnt each cntry emts→buy/sell/trde prmts→rch cntries buy prmts→still try lwer emisns→econmies nt hrt→poor cntries sell prmts→ make $ →acclrte econ. Dvlpmnt

Glbl wrmng rquirs monitrng→if humns respons rquirs intrvntn→eclgy frgle→vtal balncs mst be prtctd and prsrvd

LEARNING HOW TO
ANSWER ESSAY QUESTIONS

It's now time to complete Steps 5 and 6 of the Chewing-Up-Information system.

Step 5: Answer the *subtitle* questions. Write powerful sentences that summarize the key information. You may use your notes to answer the subtitle questions.

Begin each short essay with a **strong topic sentence.** Below you will find a sample topic sentence. You may use it if you wish when you answer the first subtitle question. It would be preferable, however, for you to make up your own topic sentence.

Sample topic sentence: Some scientists believe that human behavior is playing a major role in causing global warming.

When you've written everything that you think is important, finish your essay with a **strong concluding sentence** that ties the information together and makes a powerful statement. Below is a sample concluding sentence. You may use it, or you may prefer to make up your own concluding sentence.

Sample concluding sentence: Global warming poses a major threat to the world's ecology, and the consequences of not identifying and address- ing the factors responsible for this phenomenon could be disastrous.

Now use your notes to answer the subtitle questions using powerful topic and concluding sentences. This process will require thought and effort. With sufficient practice (and feedback from your teacher), you'll find that writing powerful topic and concluding sentences and informative essays will become easier.

Subtitle Questions

Why does human behavior have an impact on climate?

_____

_____

_____

_____

_____

_____

What causes climate changes?

_____

_____

_____

_____

_____

_____

What is the greenhouse effect?

_____

_____

_____

_____

_____

_____

_____

How can global warming be prevented?

_____

_____

_____

_____

_____

_____

_____

_____

Answering the Title Question

Step 6: Answer the title question. Your answer should be in the form of a short but comprehensive essay. You want to demonstrate that you've understood the material and can effectively incorporate and summarize the key information.

You may use your notes to answer the question, or you may want to experiment and see how much you can remember without your notes. (Of course, your teacher may give explicit instructions about whether students should or should not use their notes to write the essays.) If these subtitle questions were asked on an actual essay test, you would most likely not be allowed to use notes to answer them, unless, of course, this were an open-book test. You would have to include as much as you can remember from having studied and reviewed your notes.

Before writing an important test essay, it's a good idea to jot down quickly the important information you want to include and the important points you want to make. This outline functions as a "memory-jogger" so that you don't omit key information. You can do this brief outline (often referred to as a **thumbnail outline**) in pencil and erase it before handing it in the essay, or you can write it on a separate piece of paper. Your outline should take no more than a minute or two to complete. Although this procedure requires a little extra time, it can save time in the long run by helping you organize and sequence the information you want to include in your essay. The following is a sample thumbnail outline. For the title question: *What is global warming?*

Temp flctuates➔ntural➔cloud cvr, vlcns, snlght,

Wrmer .5 to 1.5 Fahr. last 100 yrs

Rse 3–5 Fahr by 2100?

6B tns carbn released each year➔176B 1859–1980

Incrs C atmshr➔25% + CO_2 gs snce 1880➔slwng heat escpe erth➔posble incrs gw

Hman role➔ Cnstruct & dforestn➔Eco effcts➔spcs extnct

Grnhse effct➔ntral➔warm atmsphr➔trppng gs➔photsyn CO_2 back to O➔last 2 dcds hghst temp evr rcrded➔mr C in atmsph thn lst 160,000 yrs

Nw tech➔ergy effic➔motors, etc➔cars➔lwr use fssl fuels Pln: sell prmts

Your thumbnail will help you to remember key information you want to include in your essay. *Remember:* Teachers want well-organized, well-written, persuasive essays, and they reward students who write first-rate essays with good grades!

Title Question Essay: *What is global warming?*

Write your essay on a separate piece of paper. This essay should be longer than those that answered the subtitle questions. Try to write your essay without looking at your notes. Because you will have more time to write it, you will also have more time to make up a thumbnail outline. Include all the information you think your teacher would consider important and organize the information so that it makes sense and "flows." Your goal is to impress your teacher with how much you know about the global warming and why it is such an important topic. Remember to begin with a powerful topic sentence.

When completing your essay, make sure to tie everything together with a powerful concluding sentence. When you've finished writing all the essays, compare them with the models that follow. Because you have written your essays in your own words, they will be different. Yours may even be better than those provided here! Make sure each contains the important information and has a powerful topic and concluding sentence. After comparing your essays with the models, feel free to make changes. To write effectively, you must continually work to improve your skills. You cannot develop good writing skills without practice and effort!

Model Essays

Subtitle Question: *How does human behavior have an impact on climate?*

Humans could be having a direct impact on the earth's surface temperature. The burning of fossil fuels—oil, coal, natural gas, and wood—to power cars, produce electricity, and heat homes releases CO_2 into the atmosphere. Six billion tons of carbon are emitted every year, and more than 176 billion tons have been released between 1859 and 1980. This may be responsible for the 25% increase in CO_2 in the atmosphere since 1880 and in the increase of heat-trapping gases in the atmosphere. The destruction of forests for fuel and to make way for farms, highways, towns, and cities is reducing the vegetation that transforms CO_2 into oxygen by means of photosynthesis. As habitat is destroyed, species can become extinct, and the society living in these habitats can be altered. Scientific studies indicate that as many as one-third of the 1,103 species examined could vanish by 2050. The resulting increase in heat-trapping gases could change rainfall patterns and injure ecosystems. Polar ice might melt, low-lying areas could become inundated, commerce could be damaged, and rich agricultural land could become deserts.

Subtitle Question: *Why are there natural changes in climate?*

Climate changes can have an effect on human society and on the survival of the earth's species. For example, the climate in the northern regions was once milder than today, and the Vikings were able to migrate from Iceland and establish colonies in Greenland, which actually had a much colder climate than Iceland. The temperature subsequently became colder, and the Vikings abandoned their settlements in Greenland.

Climate changes have been historically linked to natural phenomena such as cloud cover, ocean currents such as El Niño, and variations in sunlight. Volcanic eruptions can spew sulfur and ash into the atmosphere and change weather patterns. This is what happened in 1991 when Mount Pinatubo erupted in the Philippines. The temperature throughout the world was lowered by approximately 1 degree Fahrenheit. Periodic fluctuations in the earth's surface temperature that are attributable to nature are clearly facts of life on earth.

Subtitle Question: *What is the greenhouse effect?*

The greenhouse effect is a natural phenomenon. The earth is bathed in sunlight that generates heat. Some of this heat is radiated back into space. Some is absorbed by the earth's surface and is then reflected into the atmosphere where gases such as CO_2, methane, and water vapor trap the heat. Without this warming of the atmosphere, life as we know it could not exist.

The major concern is whether human behavior is causing too many heat-trapping gases to be emitted into the atmosphere and whether this behavior is altering the natural balances and accelerating global warming. Three facts are causing alarm for some scientists: (1) record high global temperature during the last two decades; (2) 1995 was the warmest year on record; and (3) the carbon content in the atmosphere is the highest in 160,000 years. If these trends continue, the greenhouse effect could become the "hothouse" effect, and earth's delicate ecology could be seriously damaged.

Subtitle Question: *How can global warming be prevented?*

Fossil fuels are burned to produce energy, and this process releases heat-trapping gases into the atmosphere. Developing new technology to increase energy efficiency would lower energy consumption and reduce the emission of heat-trapping greenhouse gases such as CO_2 into the atmosphere. Examples of new energy-saving technology include: more efficient electric motors to run air-conditioners, fans, refrigerators, and dishwashers; more efficient light bulbs; and better building insulation. Developing more efficient gasoline engines for automobiles and expanding the use of battery-powered and hybrid gasoline engine/electric motor automobiles could also play a major role in reducing the use of fossil fuels and the greenhouse gases that are being released into the atmosphere. Cars are also under development that are powered by nonfossil fuels such as hydrogen. These cars produce no heat-trapping gases.

ANSWERING THE TITLE QUESTION

Title Question: *What is global warming?*

The earth's surface temperature periodically fluctuates. At the present time, the climate on earth is becoming warmer, and the temperature during the last one hundred years has risen between .5 and 1.5 degrees Fahrenheit. During the last thirty years, the average surface temperature has increased more rapidly than at any time in recorded history. Some scientists predict that the earth's temperature might rise by 3 to 5 degrees by the year 2100. This increase could have a major destructive impact on the world's ecosystems.

Human behavior may be playing a significant role in global warming. Some scientists believe that the burning of carbon-based fuels to run factories, power cars, and heat and air-condition homes and building are adding to the CO_2 and other heat-trapping gases that are being emitted into the atmosphere. Deforestation and the construction of towns and cities that encroach on vegetation can have a major impact on photosynthesis, the process by which CO_2 is converted back into oxygen. Habitats, species, and native societies are being threatened.

Increases in the earth's surface temperature can cause polar ice to melt, raise sea levels, and cause flooding. Global warming could also increase tropical storms and alter weather patterns. This could cause agricultural areas to become deserts.

Changes in climate are naturally occurring phenomena, and cloud cover, sunlight, ocean currents such as El Niño, and volcanic eruptions can cause these changes. Human behavior may also be a major factor. In the last two decades, record high annual global temperatures have been recorded, and 1995 was the warmest year on record. The carbon content in the atmosphere is higher than at any time during the last 160,000 years. The risks to our ecosystems and the delicate balances that exist in nature are obvious. Global warming is clearly a legitimate concern. Unless the role that human beings may be playing in increasing the earth's temperature is fully understood and unless solutions to the problem are devised, our planet and its ecology could be seriously damaged.

DISTINGUISHING MAIN IDEAS FROM DETAILS

It's now time to learn the final step (Step 7) of the Chewing-Up-Information system. After you've completed taking notes and you've answered the subtitle and main idea questions, you will want to *review your notes at least one time before taking a test.* To help you review, read through your notes and use two highlighters or pencils of different colors. Highlight or underscore main idea information in one color and detail information in the other color. An example of **main idea information:** *Brnng carbn-based fossil fuels→CO_2 rleased.* It is a main idea because some scientists consider the emission of CO_2 into the atmosphere to be a major factor responsible for global warming. An example of **detail information:** *6B tns of crbn emtted each yr atmsphr.*

Step 7: Differentiate the main ideas from the details (or facts) in your notes. Use highlighters or colored pencils. Choose one color for details and one for main ideas. Use these same colors whenever you review your notes in any subject. If you don't have highlighters or colored pencils, use a standard pencil for details and a pen for main ideas. For practice, go through your notes now and highlight or underline the main ideas and details. You must then decide which information must be memorized. (Techniques for doing so are examined in the next unit.)

REVIEW OF HOW TO TAKE
AND USE TEXTBOOK NOTES

	True	False
Turn the title into a question before reading material.	_____	_____
Turn each subtitle into question before reading material.	_____	_____
Answer the title question before reading material.	_____	_____
Answer subtitle questions before taking notes	_____	_____
Speed-read material after taking notes.	_____	_____
When speed-reading, read every word very carefully.	_____	_____
After speed-reading, read the material again more carefully.	_____	_____
Write down key information in note form while reading carefully.	_____	_____
Include words such as "the" "a" and "of" in notes.	_____	_____
Use abbreviations whenever possible.	_____	_____
Highlight or underline in your textbooks.	_____	_____
When reviewing, highlight details in one color and main ideas in another color.	_____	_____

REVIEW OF HOW TO USE
ESSAY QUESTIONS AS A STUDY TOOL

	True	False
After taking notes, answer the main idea title question with an essay.	_____	_____
After taking notes, answer each main idea subtitle question with a short essay.	_____	_____
The last step in the note-taking process is to answer the title question.	_____	_____
Before writing an essay on a test, make a quick thumbnail outline to organize information and make certain you include everything you know about the subject.	_____	_____

Unit 9

Power Studying

For Teachers

Objectives

This unit reinforces and expands the study techniques taught in Units 6–8 and integrates these techniques into a comprehensive test preparation methodology.

LESSON PLAN

1. After reading the introductory anecdote in **What to Study and How to Study,** students consider what information teachers are likely to consider important when they make up tests and what they would want students to understand and remember. After reviewing the previously taught seven steps of the **Chewing-Up-Information** system, students add two additional steps: composing and answering short-answer detail questions.

2. Students produce and answer short-answer, true–false, and multiple-choice about the global warming unit introduced in Unit 8.

3. Students discover that by their having already turned the subtitles and the title of the global warming unit into questions, they've created a list of potential essay questions that they can use to prepare for a test.

4. In **Jolting Your Memory,** students review the traditional methods for memorizing information.

5. In **Making Powerful Associations,** students learn a powerful alternative to traditional methods for memorizing facts and data (i.e., repetitive reading, writing, subvocalization, vocalization).

6. In **How Teachers Design Tests,** students are encouraged to make up practice tests as a final step in their studying process. They learn how to develop test-taking "radar" that helps them anticipate the test questions that their teachers are likely to ask. This activity reinforces the Chewing-Up-Information system. Students design a test based on the questions posed in the previous exercises. They then complete a test-preparation checklist that incorporates all the study techniques presented in the program. The goal is for them to make the methodical checking-off procedure the final "covering all the bases" step in their study process.

DEVELOPING TEST-TAKING RADAR

Highly motivated students who are intent on getting good grades are prepared to do whatever is necessary when preparing for tests. They carefully read the material in their textbooks, take notes, identify important details and concepts, and make every effort to comprehend the content. They also develop an effective individualized method for **recalling key information.** Realizing that they can improve their grades on tests by anticipating the questions that their teachers are likely to ask, they often pose questions as they study and make certain that they can answer these questions.

Successful, strategically minded students deliberately train themselves to think like their teacher when they study. Based on their previous test experiences and on clues provided in class, they determine whether their teacher is primarily detail-oriented (i.e., emphasizes facts and typically asks multiple-choice, true-false, and short-answer questions) or concept-oriented (i.e., emphasizes ideas and issues and typically asks essay questions). Once they identify their teachers' testing preferences, they adjust their study procedure accordingly. If they conclude that their teacher emphasizes both facts and concepts on tests, they make certain that they cover all the bases.

MEMORIZING DATA

Teachers frequently require students to assimilate and memorize vast quantities of information. The data might include historical dates, spelling words, chemical formulas, math formulas, grammar rules, foreign language verb conjugations, and vocabulary definitions. For students with good visual recall, memorizing this information is relatively easy. For those with poor recall, the process can be excruciatingly difficult, painful, and demoralizing.

Students who have difficulty memorizing written information are usually at a significant disadvantage in our secondary educational system. These students may be as bright as classmates who memorize visual information with relative ease, but they may struggle to assimilate and recall facts that they consciously or unconsciously perceive as irrelevant.

The ability to recall visual information is especially critical in elementary school, when children are bombarded with copious data that they're required to absorb and store for future reference. For example, fourth-graders are expected to remember that $9 \times 9 = 81$, that there are fifty states in the union, that the capital of the United States is Washington, D.C., and that there are three branches of government. They are also expected to remember that "dismantle" means to take apart and that "famine" means a long period during which there is little or no food available. Students who can recall this type of information are usually rewarded with good grades.

Students who have good visual memory skills typically do well on tests that emphasize the retention of facts, dates, and formulas. Because they can usually "see" words in their mind, they are also better spellers (see learning styles and preferences in Unit 1). Auditory learners, on the other hand, usually try to sound out words and may be confounded by the many phonetic exceptions and pronunciation deviations in the English language. Although auditory learners are at a disadvantage when the memorization of visual information is emphasized, these students can usually capitalize on their preferred learning modality in upper-level classes in which a great deal of course content is communicated verbally in lectures and seminars.

Given the countless academic challenges that require the ability to recall visual information, all students—irrespective of their natural learning style and preferences—should ideally be taught methods for improving their visual memory skills. Those who apply these memorization methods and who are also in the habit of posing and answering questions when they study are proactively improving the likelihood of their earning good grades on exams.

Strategically minded students intuitively figure out how to compensate in areas in which they lack natural facility and deliberately develop and apply a wide range of personalized study tools when they prepare for tests. For example, a strategic student preparing for a French test might visualize herself talking to a waiter in a French restaurant while using the dialogues, vocabulary, and verbs appearing in the textbook unit she's studying. To enhance her recall, she might "hear" herself saying the phrases in her mind and using the assigned verbs and grammar, or she may practice and reinforce mastery by actually saying the words, phrases, and idioms aloud when she studies. By deliberately making the material relevant, using practical methods to improve retention, and actively and creatively engaging herself in the learning process, she significantly improves the likelihood of her mastering the content.

SUMMARY OF STUDENT EXERCISES AND ACTIVITIES

What to Study and How to Study

For many passive learners, taking a test is like shooting baskets blindfolded. If they're lucky, some shots might hit the backboard or even the rim. Few, if any, however, are actually likely to go through the hoop.

This exercise underscores the value of purposefully thinking about what information teachers are likely to consider important, what they want students to remember, and what questions they are likely to ask on a test. Students are guided to three key insights: By preparing strategically, asking penetrating questions while they study, and involving themselves actively in the study process, they can significantly increase the likelihood of their receiving good grades on tests.

Thinking Like a Teacher: Answering Short-Answer Detail and True-False Questions

This exercise further reinforces the procedure of anticipating the types of questions that are likely to be encountered on tests. By deliberately making up the same types of questions while they study and answering these questions, students can hone their test-taking radar and better comprehend and recall the content.

Thinking Like a Teacher: Answering Multiple-Choice Questions

Students can count on having to deal with countless multiple-choice tests throughout their education. Those who make a habit of developing and answering multiple-choice questions that cover the material they're studying are likely to have less difficulty handling this type of test. The goal of this exercise is to encourage students to make the procedure of composing and answering practice multiple-choice questions an integral component of their exam-preparation process.

Please note: Students have already practiced creating and answering essay questions in preceding units. In Steps 2 and 5 of the Chewing-Up-Information system (see Unit 7), they turned the title and subtitles into questions, and they then answered the questions. This is a highly effective essay test preparation procedure because the questions students pose are likely to be similar to the ones their teachers would include on a test.

Jolting Your Memory

This section helps students realize that traditional methods for memorizing important course content may not be sufficient for them. This leads to the introduction of a powerful visual association technique that can significantly enhance students' ability to retain information that is written in their textbooks and notes.

Making Powerful Associations: The Association and Visualization Technique

This section teaches students how to improve their memory by intentionally creating powerful visual images and "hooks." Students learn how to use their eyes like the lens of camera and how to imprint visual information on their brains in much the same way that images are imprinted on a chip in a digital camera. By learning to move their eyes intentionally into the upper quadrant when they're memorizing visual information, students can tap into the brain's natural mechanism for accessing and representing visual information. Colored pens or markers can be used to enhance their recall and help them create vivid images.

Making powerful visual associations, seeing information in their "mind's eye," and applying their imagination and creativity when memorizing formulas, definitions, dates, symbols, and facts provide students with powerful tools to appreciably augment their visual memory capabilities. To further improve their recall, students learn how to create powerful visual associations, and they practice the three steps of the Association and Visualization Technique with a wide range of data they might typically be required to memorize in school.

These activities require guidance, modeling, monitoring, practice, and class discussion. Having students work in small cooperative learning groups can be an effective method for facilitating mastery of the visualization procedures. Students who "get it" can help those who are having more difficulty assimilating the techniques.

How Teachers Design Tests

Many marginally performing students give little or no thought to the issues that teachers consider when making up tests. This obliviousness to the correspondence between course content and test questions considerably reduces the likelihood of these students getting good grades.

This section underscores the logical congruity between content and test questions and makes students more aware of the process teachers go through when devising tests. To reinforce this awareness, students create their own twenty-five-question test that covers the global warming unit. The two goals of the exercise are to impress on students that they can target and usually anticipate the information that is likely to be covered on their teachers' tests and that they can systematically prepare themselves for the types of questions that are likely to be asked.

Test Preparation Checklist

This exercise offers additional opportunities for students to practice "thinking like a teacher" and helps students make the process of asking questions while studying and reviewing an integral component in their test preparation. The checklist encourages students to make certain they've performed all of the steps that are requisite to effective studying. This "final countdown" is designed to verify that they've indeed studied effectively and strategically and that they're well-prepared. This verification procedure can significantly reduce test anxiety and build test-taking self-confidence.

Unit 9

Power Studying

For Students

WHAT TO STUDY AND HOW TO STUDY

The countdown to the history test had begun. Alison desperately wanted at least a B+ on the test, and she was determined to use all the new study methods she had learned. Her teacher announced the chapter test would be on Friday and would cover the unit about the French Revolution. Alison had already taken notes, but she decided it would be smart to spend some extra time mind-mapping the unit as an additional review.

It was now Monday, and Alison had only four days to prepare for the test. Realizing the clock was ticking, she put her study strategy into high gear. That evening, she reviewed her textbook notes and wrote short essays to answer the subtitle questions from the chapter. Then she answered the main idea question about the chapter title. She made sure her essays were well-organized with good topic sentences and concluding sentences. She also made sure she included all the key information from her notes.

On Tuesday night, Alison reviewed her lecture notes and her textbook notes using two highlight pens. She marked the main ideas in yellow and the details in blue.

On Wednesday, Alison used the memory technique her teacher had shown the class. She followed the three steps as she visualized and memorized the important names, facts, and dates that she had written on index cards.

It was now time for the final effort. On Thursday evening, Alison made up practice multiple-choice, true-false, and short-answer questions about the unit and made sure she could answer them.

Having completed this last step, Alison felt confident that she had done everything she could to prepare. She was as ready as she could possibly be!

STUDYING FOR TESTS

Your final preparation procedure can make the difference between a good grade on a test and a mediocre or even poor grade. By studying smart, mind-mapping, and taking the time to use the Chewing-Up-Information system, you can significantly improve the likelihood that your test grades will improve.

Let's review what you already know about studying smart. You've learned how to

1. Speed-read

2. Mind-map

3. Ask title and subtitle questions

4. Take notes

5. Answer questions about the title and subtitles

6. Study your notes and highlight main ideas and details

Two other important steps can significantly improve your test performance and your self-confidence.

1. Think about the information your teacher is likely to consider important and spend extra time reviewing this information.

2. Make up practice multiple-choice, true–false, and short-answer test questions.

Some teachers will want you to learn and memorize important facts and details. They might ask the following type of question on a test: "How many tons of carbon are currently being emitted each year into the atmosphere?"

Other teachers want you to understand concepts and main ideas. They might ask the following essay question on a test: "Discuss how human beings may be causing significant changes to the earth's climate."

If your teachers usually ask detail questions on tests, it would make sense to make up a list of important **details and facts** while studying. You've already highlighted these details in your notes. This step requires extra study time, but it can help you to do better on the test. You might write these important facts on large index cards and begin reviewing whenever you have some free time. You could study the information on the school bus or while you're eating breakfast.

Identifying the important information in your notes is only the first step. The next step is to figure out **a method for remembering the facts and details.** Unless you have a great memory, reading over the list a few times will not be enough. To memorize a great deal of information, you need to use powerful memory techniques. You'll learn these techniques later in this unit.

THINKING LIKE A TEACHER

Answering Short-Answer Detail Questions

Refer back to your notes on global warming. Make up ten **short-answer detail** questions from the global warming unit. For example: *In what year was the highest annual temperature on earth recorded?* Some of the questions you make up may require a one-word or one-date answer. Other may require a sentence to answer. (*Please note:* If you were actually preparing for a test covering the global warming unit, you would certainly want to make up more that ten detail questions.)

Detail Questions

1. _____

2. _____

3. _____

4. _____

5. _____

6. _____

7. _____

8. _____

9. _____

10. _____

Now answer your own questions!

Answers

1. _____

2. _____

3. _____

4. _____

5. _____

6. _____

7. _____

8. _____

9. _____

10. _____

Answering True-False Questions

When teachers want their students to understand and recall facts and details from the material they're studying, they often give tests that contain true-false questions. For practice, make up ten true-false questions from the global warming unit. To make this easier, you could make some minor alterations in the short-answer questions you made up on the previous page and change them to true-false questions. For example: *In 1972, monitoring devices to measure the gases in the atmosphere were first positioned in Hawaii at an altitude of 11,000 feet.* **TRUE   FALSE**

True-False Questions

1. _____

   TRUE FALSE

2. _____

   TRUE FALSE

3. _____

   TRUE FALSE

4. _____

   TRUE FALSE

5. _____

   TRUE FALSE

6. _____

   TRUE FALSE

7. _____

   TRUE FALSE

8. _____

TRUE   FALSE

9. _____

TRUE   FALSE

10. _____

TRUE   FALSE

Answering Multiple-Choice Questions

Another way for teachers to determine whether their students understand and remember facts and details is to ask multiple-choice questions on tests. Because these tests focus on details and subtle issues, students often complain that the questions are intentionally "tricky." To improve your performance on multiple-choice tests, practice making up ten questions from information in the global warming unit. For example:

Global warming

    a. could reduce the volume of water in the world's oceans.
    b. could increase the polar icepack.
    c. could alter rainfall patterns.
    d. could be beneficial for agricultural production.

Multiple-Choice Questions

1. _____

    a. _____

    b. _____

    c. _____

    d. _____

2. _____

    a. _____

    b. _____

    c. _____

    d. _____

3. _____

    a. _____

    b. _____

    c. _____

    d. _____

4. _____

    a. _____

    b. _____

    c. _____

    d. _____

5. _____

    a. _____

    b. _____

    c. _____

    d. _____

6. _____

    a. _____

    b. _____

    c. _____

    d. _____

7. _____

    a. _____

    b. _____

    c. _____

    d. _____

8. _____

    a. _____

    b. _____

    c. _____

    d. _____

9. _____

    a. _____

    b. _____

    c. _____

    d. _____

10. _____

    a. _____

    b. _____

    c. _____

    d. _____

Now answer your own multiple-choice questions without looking at your notes!

JOLTING YOUR MEMORY

Have you ever thought about all the information you've memorized in your life? Let's look at some examples:

Your address

Your telephone number

Your zip code

The words to many of your favorite songs

The date Columbus arrived in North America

The Pledge of Allegiance

The multiplication tables

The name of the first president of the United States

The spelling of the word "through"

You may not realize you're constantly memorizing information. Because you've heard about George Washington so many times, you know he was the first president of the United States without having to think about it. If you hadn't memorized your multiplication tables and if you didn't know that $6 \times 6 = 36$, you wouldn't be able to divide 6 into 360,000.

Students do not all memorize information in the same way. Some of the most common methods include the following:

1. Writing information over and over until you memorize it

2. Saying information aloud over and over until you memorize it

3. Reading something over and over until you memorize it

4. Making a picture or word association with the information

You've undoubtedly already used Techniques 1–3 many times when studying for tests. Let's take a look at Technique 4—**making an association.** This method is a powerful memory tool and could be of great help to you when you have to memorize vocabulary words, foreign language conjugations, chemical formulas, or facts from a textbook or from your notes. In the section that follows, you'll learn how to use this tool.

MAKING POWERFUL ASSOCIATIONS

Look at the following definitions and sample sentences:
   deprecate: to attach little importance, disparage, or cheapen
   During the debates, the candidate has repeatedly deprecated his opponent's political agenda and has implied that his rival is incompetent.
   ascend: to go up
   *The director told the actor to **ascend** the stairs with a happy smile on his face.*
   preconception: prejudice, bias, or notion
   The coach had a preconception that smaller athletes could not play football well, and Justin was determined to prove him wrong.
   idiosyncrasy: a strange behavior or mannerism
   *They laughed at the comedian because of his **idiosyncrasies**.*
   buoyant: able to float
   *The new design made the boat very **buoyant**.*
   flamboyant: showy, ostentatious
   *The actor's clothing was very **flamboyant**.*

An effective method for remembering these words is to make a visual association between the word and its meaning and then to see the word, the definition, and the association "in your mind." This is called the **Association and Visualization Technique**. Let's practice the technique.

THE ASSOCIATION AND VISUALIZATION TECHNIQUE

Step 1: Write the word and the definition for each word on a file card or piece of paper. Put only one word and definition on each card. Write each word using a different color felt pen or pencil. Write the definition in another color.

Step 2: After writing down the word and definition, create a picture in your mind that uses the word. "See" this image clearly. For example, you might visualize a political debate. In your mind, *see* two candidates debating as they stand at their respective podiums on the stage of an auditorium that is filled with people. One candidate is wearing a gray suit and a red tie. (Choose any colors you wish.) The other candidate is wearing a white blouse, a navy blue jacket, pearl earrings, and a pearl necklace. See the candidate in the gray suit and red tie point at his opponent as he mean-spiritedly deprecates her ideas and accomplishments. Choose a *powerful* image to help you "take a picture" of the scene and help you remember the meaning of the word. Follow the same procedure with the next word. After writing down the word and its definition, you might visualize a big black dog running up some stairs. In your mind's eye, see the dog *ascend* the steps.

Step 3: Keep looking at the card until you can actually "see" the word and its definition not only through your eyes, but also in your mind. Try to see the word (for example, *buoyant*) in your mind written in the color you've selected. Now close your eyes and actually **visualize** the image you associated with the word and the definition written in color on the *inside of your eyelids*. If you can't remember them, open your eyes and study them again. When you are ready, try to see the word and definition again. When you can, write them on a piece of paper. Use the same procedure with the next word and definition.

Taping or tacking the index card slightly above your head will help you use the visualization technique. Experiment with taping the card slightly to the left or the right of your nose above eye level. Decide whether the card "feels" better to the right or the left of your eyes. By looking up as you memorize the word and seeing the image that you've associated with the word, you'll be able to imprint the information more effectively in your mind. The brain retains visual data better when the eyes are directed upward while the information is being learned.

This method of linking information (definitions, spelling words, dates, number, facts, etc.) with visual images and seeing these images in your mind should work with anything you have to memorize in a history, foreign language, science, or English class. Always choose colors you like! When studying vocabulary definitions or a foreign language, create sentences that incorporate the words or grammar and then create images you can see vividly in your mind. (For example, visualize a *buoyant* cork bobbing in the water.)

Sometimes the material in a particular subject doesn't allow you to form a vivid mental picture. For example, the chemical symbol *Na* represents sodium.

You may not be able to visualize what sodium actually looks like. You may simply need to imprint Na = sodium in your mind's eye without forming a vivid visual picture of the actual chemical. You might also want to see a bottle of white powder floating in the air with the letters *Na* printed in large letters on the label and the word "sodium" printed below.

Try an experiment. Use the Association and Visualization Technique with the following chemical symbols. After you've used the method and feel you've learned the symbols, test yourself and see if you've remembered them.

H_2O = water (Perhaps you might visualize a flowing stream on which a paper boat is floating. On the side of the boat, the chemical symbol H_2O is written in green or red letters.)

C = carbon

CO = carbon monoxide (produced by a car engine)

CO_2 = carbon dioxide (produced by lungs when breathing)

H = hydrogen

O = oxygen

Na = sodium

Cl = chlorine

Fe = iron

He = helium

Pb = lead

N = nitrogen

HCl = hydrochloric acid

NaCl = salt

You can also use the visualizing method to remember math facts. Look at the math facts that follow and, after studying each one, close your eyes and see it in color in your mind. See $12 \times 12 = 144$ "printed" on your closed eyelids. Use this color imprinting technique to help you remember the following multiplication facts.

$12 \times 12 = 144$	$16 \times 16 = 256$
$13 \times 13 = 169$	$17 \times 17 = 309$
$14 \times 14 = 196$	$18 \times 18 = 324$
$15 \times 15 = 225$	$19 \times 19 = 361$

Now use the visualization method to memorize how to spell these difficult words. Remember to imprint the word deliberately in your mind's eye. With your eyes closed, you want to see the letters of each word in color on the back of your eyelids.

prerogative (definition: option)

losing

sobriquet (definition: nickname)

lieutenant

sergeant

colonel

effervescent (definition: bubbly)

circuitry

HOW TEACHERS DESIGN TESTS

You may think that making up a test is easy for teachers. Creating a fair test that covers a history or science unit actually requires a great deal of time and thought on the teacher's part. Below are some issues teachers must consider when making up a test.

1. What information is important in this chapter?

2. What do I want my students to understand and remember?

3. How do I find out if my students have understood and assimilated the important information?

4. How can I ask questions that are challenging but fair?

By training yourself to think like a teacher when you study, you can increase the chances that you'll be able to anticipate what your teachers are likely to ask on tests. This gives you a big advantage over students who do not know how to identify the information their teachers are likely to consider important when they study.

Unless the school year has just begun, you probably know a great deal about how your teachers think. You've already taken their tests, and you've spent many hours together in the classroom. By reviewing the types of questions they've asked on previous tests and the kinds of information they emphasize in class discussions, you could probably anticipate what they would most likely ask on a test covering the French Revolution or nuclear energy.

If it's the beginning of the school year and you don't yet have a sense about your teachers' testing methods, you will need to become extra observant and make mental notes about the types of questions that appear on tests. Analyze your teachers' typical questions, testing style (multiple choice, short answer, true-false, essay), and primary orientation (details or concepts) and begin to make strategic adjustments in your study strategy.

There's a powerful studying "trick" you can use to prepare for tests. It's quite simple: **Make up your own test!** This should be the last step after you have completed your studying.

In exercises at the beginning of this unit, you made up short-answer, true-false, and multiple choice questions about global warming. As you made up these questions, you probably used your notes or mind-map.

Refer back to the thinking-like-a-teacher exercise on pages 182–186. On a separate piece of paper, make up a practice test consisting of twenty-five questions. Select questions you think your science teacher would ask on a unit test. For example:

1. Based on current trends, by how many degrees do concerned scientists believe the temperature might rise by 2100?

2. Describe four ways in which humans may be playing a role in changing the climate.

   _____

   _____

   _____

   _____

3. A modern-day natural phenomenon that affected global temperature was a volcano on _____ in the Philippines in _____.

4. Approximately how many tons of carbon are being emitted into the atmosphere each year as the result of the combustion of fossil fuels?
   A. 6 million
   B. 60 million
   C. 600 million
   D. 6 billion

5. The Vikings established settlements in Greenland because the weather had become colder. **True False**

Use the previous questions as a model when you make up your test. Try not to use the same questions. If you're having difficulty making up questions, you can make minor changes and use the sample questions to get started. As you make up the test, remember to consider what your teacher would want you to know and remember.

The Payoffs of Thinking Like a Teacher

Teachers go through the same process you've just gone through when making up tests. If you get in the habit of thinking like your teachers and make up practice tests, your grades will improve. *Good test preparation requires strategic thinking and planning.*

Of course, you may discover questions on tests that you did not anticipate. Although this can be upsetting, you can learn from this experience. Try to figure out *why* your teacher considered this particular information important. The next time you study, make adjustments and fine-tune your test preparation radar.

Good students are rarely surprised with they take a test. Because they've *done their homework,* they usually know in advance most of the questions that their teacher are likely to ask.

TEST PREPARATION CHECKLIST

As you prepare for tests, use the checklist on page 193 to help you decide whether you've done everything that needs to be done. Completing all the steps certifies you're thinking and studying smart. The Study Max steps require some extra time and effort, but if you use the techniques consistently, you'll be rewarded with better grades. Each time you apply the methods, you'll discover that the procedures will become easier to use. Before long, you'll be using the procedures automatically.

Learning to study is like learning gymnastics. If you have sufficient desire and train hard, you'll become more proficient, motivated, and self-confident. This same phenomenon also applies to studying. If you study effectively and work conscientiously, your grades and test-taking confidence will improve. You'll realize that your hard work is paying off, and this will motivate you to increase your effort. Your accomplishments will enhance your positive feelings about yourself and your abilities, and you'll discover that you're in a success cycle. This cycle can be graphically represented as follows.

Success/Motivation Cycle

Notice that the arrows point in two directions. Success produces effort, and effort produces success. Positive feelings produce motivation, and motivation produces positive feelings. Effort produces success and motivation. Each component in the loop affects the other components.

Test Preparation Checklist

	YES	NO
Before reading the assigned material, I turn the main title into a question.	___	___
I speed-read the content at least once.	___	___
I mind-map and/or take traditional notes.	___	___
I answer the subtitle and main idea questions.	___	___
I identify the main ideas and details in my notes.	___	___
I use the association and visualization technique to help me remember important information.	___	___
I review previous tests to get a sense of the teacher's style and orientation.	___	___
I carefully review my notes and the textbook before a test.	___	___
I try to predict the questions my teacher is likely to ask on a test.	___	___
I make up a practice test.	___	___
I study with a friend or friends when appropriate.	___	___

If you do all of the steps on the preceding checklist when preparing for a test, you should congratulate yourself. You're doing first-rate job of studying. You're **thinking and studying smart!** In the final unit in this book, you'll tie together *all* the thinking and studying skills you've learned in the **Study Max Program.**

WHAT YOU HAVE LEARNED
ABOUT STUDYING

Connect the statements by drawing a line from column 1 to column 2:

Taking notes	powerful sentence that begins an essay
Turning title into a question	helps you organize information
Turning subtitle into a question	final sentence in an essay that ties everything together
Writing answers to questions	method for remembering and understanding what you have read
Topic sentence	helps you prepare for a test
Seeing information in your mind	helps you think about the content
Concluding sentence	helps you focus on the content of a section you are studying
Thumbnail outline	helps you make up practice test questions
Thinking like a teacher	a good way to study smart
Identifying main ideas and details	helps you identify important information, represent facts visually and creatively, and understand how information is connected
Making up practice tests	provides a quick overview of the content.
Speed-reading	helps you organize your essay
Mind-mapping	helps you memorize

Unit 10

Creating a Master Plan for Studying

For Teachers

Objectives

This unit provides opportunities for students to review, practice, integrate, and apply the entire range of studying principles they've learned in the preceding units.

LESSON PLAN

1. After reading the introductory anecdote, **Covering All the Bases**, students critically examine Elena's study plan and recommend specific strategic study techniques that could improve her academic performance.

2. Students do a three-part studying experiment. They integrate the study skills they have learned, develop a master study plan, and keep track of their school performance for two weeks. This is a more comprehensive experiment than the one done in the activity **Reducing Distraction,** because students are now being asked to apply all of the study methods they've learned during the course of the experiment. (See "A Sheltered Study Island" in Unit 5.)

3. In **Being Relaxed When You Take Tests,** students learn techniques for reducing their test-taking anxiety, fear, and stress.

4. Students examine an illustration of a student who is clearly studying efficiently and identify the positive study practices they observe.

THE OVERLAPPING COMPONENTS OF PRODUCTIVE STUDYING

Mastery and assimilation of good study skills requires repeated opportunities for practice and application. The goal is for students to apply these skills automatically. Once students realize that they possess the requisite resources to achieve scholastically, their academic self-confidence will improve, and they'll be more predisposed to use the tools that can ensure continued achievement. The core premise of the **Study Max Program** is that effective study skills in tandem with motivation, effort, and perseverance will produce improved performance. This improvement will stimulate the desire for more success, which, in turn, will stimulate additional motivation, effort, and perseverance. Success is addictive. Once students taste it, they'll want more.

SUMMARY OF STUDENT EXERCISES AND ACTIVITIES

Covering All the Bases

The introductory case study encapsulates most of the specific procedures that have been systematically taught in the Study Max Program and provides a quick and painless review. Students examine a conscientious student's focused and comprehensive test preparation plan and the practical methods she uses to control her test anxiety. This content and the two short exercises that follow lend themselves to a dynamic class discussion about productive study procedures.

Examining the Story

Students methodically identify, underline, and number each technique that Elena used to prepare for the exam. For the purposes of review and reinforcement, they then write down each of the sixteen identified procedures.

Evaluating and Predicting

Students evaluate the efficacy of Elena's study plan and make predictions about the outcome and long-range implications of her test preparation methods. The objective of this exercise is for students to recognize that Elena has intentionally implemented systematic study measures that appreciably increase the likelihood of her getting a good grade on the test.

Expanding the Study Plan

Students are asked to make suggestions about how Elena's study plan might be further enhanced. The objective of this exercise is to impress on students that even a good methodology can be revised and expanded so that it becomes an even better.

This exercise is intended to serve as a catalyst for a dynamic class discussion and a review of the entire gamut of study and organizational methods that have been presented in the program. It would, however, be unrealistic to expect all students to consistently apply every method that has been taught. To do so would require a time commitment that many teenagers, and especially those who are not college oriented, would consider excessive. Rather, the goal is to guide students to the realization that they now have access to a range of powerful study tools that they can use to improve their grades. Ideally, your students will elect to use the methods that are reasonable and appropriate in each situation.

During the class discussion, it might prove beneficial to interject a sports analogy to which many students can relate. Just as a golfer must select the best club to make a particular shot, so, too, must students select the best combination of study methods when preparing for tests. You want your students to analyze carefully each challenge they face. You want them to be aware of their options in responding to the challenge, and you want them to recognize the importance of making astute choices. You also want your students to realize that to do well in school, they must deliberately design a well-conceived, comprehensive, and individualized study strategy.

Being Relaxed When You Take Tests

Most students experience varying degrees of test anxiety. It goes with the territory of being in school and having to take exams. In extreme cases, the anxiety can erect a formidable barrier to getting good grades. Even highly motivated, conscientious, achievement-oriented students may become so overwrought by their own intensity that they "clutch" during a test and forget much of what they've learned. Stress and fear of failure can be especially debilitating for students who have had an extensive track record of marginal test performance. These students may study diligently and effectively and may know the material "backward and forward." Their anticipatory stress and, in some cases, actual panic when taking a test can cause their brain to shut down and torpedo their performance.

The objective of this exercise is to impress on students that they have options for handling their apprehension. Once they discover that practical relaxation techniques can help them assume proactive control of their test anxiety, they'll feel less vulnerable and more academically self-confident. With their angst under control, they'll be able to function at a level that is commensurate with their actual mastery of the content.

Testing Your Master Study Plan

In this activity, students apply the strategic thinking, planning, and organizational skills they've learned. They practice checking off specific study procedures each day. The objective is for students to continue monitoring themselves, keeping track of their grades, and applying the thinking and study techniques they have practiced. To defuse potential resistance to this methodical checking-off procedure, impress on students that once they establish the habit of monitoring themselves, they may elect to keep track of their performance mentally without having to check off each study procedure on a formal list.

Some Final Words

The intent of this final segment is to heighten your students' awareness of the applicability and functionality of what they've learned. The nuts and bolts of productive studying are succinctly revisited, and students are encouraged to use the study techniques that they've methodically practiced and systematically assimilated.

You may have taught all of the study techniques presented in the program, or, because of limited time, you may have selected specific units to teach. In the latter case, it's recommended that you make copies of the units that haven't been covered in class available to motivated students to complete on their own. The message of this final segment is crystal clear: Once students get into the habit of succeeding academically, they will become addicted to achievement. Unlike deleterious addictions, this particular habit is wholesome and beneficial.

You may conclude that your students would benefit from expanding their skills and from learning additional strategic and critical thinking procedures that will enhance the likelihood of their being able to prevail not only in school, but also in the world beyond school. These topics are addressed in a companion Corwin program titled **Life Success Skills** (forthcoming).

Unit 10

Creating a Master Plan for Studying

For Students

COVERING ALL THE BASES

Elena closed her eyes as she waited for the chemistry final to be handed out. Despite having studied for a total of twelve hours, she was still nervous. The teacher had told the class that the test would count for 35 percent of the semester grade. Fortunately, Elena had received good grades on the weekly quizzes, the midterm, her lab reports, and the homework assignments. If she could just get a minimum of a B+ on the final, she would get an A– in the course. If she got an A or even an A– on the final, she would get an A in the course.

Elena had started reviewing for the exam two weeks earlier. She took notes from her textbook, and she had mind-mapped some of the difficult sections to help her better understand the information. Of course, Elena had also taken lecture notes. In preparing for the exam, she had carefully reread her notes as well as the assigned chapters in her textbook. As she studied, she made up practice test questions. Although it had been challenging, Elena had kept to her study schedule and had spent one hour studying every school night. The evening before the exam, she and Tanya had spent three hours studying together. They reviewed previous quizzes and tests, asked each other questions, and tried to identify the information that their teacher was likely to consider important. Each girl made up a practice test for the other. After taking the test, they discussed their answers.

Although still anxious, Elena was convinced that she was as prepared as she could possibly be. She felt confident that she would do well on the exam, assuming that she didn't panic and forget what she had studied. While waiting for the test to be distributed, Elena took several deep breaths with her eyes closed and reminded herself that she knew the material. She focused her mind on the spot where her tension was most intense—her solar plexus. She then imagined opening a valve and letting all of the stress and anxiety slowly ebb from her body. This procedure, which only required about a minute, made her feel much calmer.

The teacher made several announcements and finally, after what seemed like an eternity, he distributed the exam. When Elena received her copy, she quickly glanced over the questions and breathed a sigh of relief. She realized that she'd be able to answer all of them. The twelve hours she had spent studying had paid off! Now, she had to remind herself not to get *too* confident because she knew that whenever she did, she tended to make silly mistakes. Forty minutes later, Elena left the classroom with a smile of relief on her face.

EXAMINING THE STORY

Elena had a very powerful study strategy that consisted of sixteen specific steps. Carefully identify and number each of the steps. See if you can find the sixteen steps. (In some cases, more than one step is included in a single sentence.) Once you have numbered each step, write them below.

Step 1: _____

Step 2: _____

Step 3: _____

Step 4: _____

Step 5: _____

Step 6: _____

Step 7: _____

Step 8: _____

Step 9: _____

Step 10: _____

Step 11: _____

Step 12: _____

Step 13: _____

Step 14: _____

Step 15: _____

Step 16: _____

EVALUATING AND PREDICTING

How would you evaluate the overall effectiveness of Elena's study plan?

1	2	3	4	5	6	7	8	9	10
Not Effective			**Fairly Effective**				**Very Effective**		

Base on the description of Elena's study plan, what grade do you think she'll receive on the final exam? _____

Would you be willing to study as conscientiously as Elena to get a good grade on a final exam? **Yes No Not Sure**

How many hours maximum would you be prepared to study for a final exam?

_____

On the basis of what you've read about Elena in the case study, make some predictions.

Her overall GPA when she graduates high school will be _____ .

The likelihood of her going to a two- or four-year college or university:

1	2	3	4	5	6	7	8	9	10
Not Likely			**Fairly Likely**				**Very Likely**		

The likelihood of her being successful in college:

1	2	3	4	5	6	7	8	9	10
Not Likely			**Fairly Likely**				**Very Likely**		

The likelihood of her being successful in her career:

1	2	3	4	5	6	7	8	9	10
Not Likely			**Fairly Likely**				**Very Likely**		

MAKING ENHANCEMENTS

Have you ever heard the expression, "If it ain't broke, don't fix it"? Well, even a good system can be improved. Automobile and electronic manufacturers are continually trying to make their products even better. Can you think of any other steps Elena might have taken in preparing for the exam? List ideas that were not mentioned in the story. For example, she could study sitting at a desk or table. Review in your mind all of the smart-studying steps that you've learned and practiced. Write down these additional study improvement ideas.

Step 17: _____

Step 18: _____

Step 19: _____

Step 20: _____

Step 21: _____

Step 22: _____

Step 23: _____

BEING RELAXED WHEN YOU TAKE TESTS

Some students do an excellent job of studying but panic when they take tests. Because of their fear and anxiety, their grades do not accurately reflect how much they actually learned and how much time they spent preparing for the exam.

Having to take a test can cause stress and anxiety for anyone, and it can be especially stressful if you really want to do well but have some doubts about your skill, ability, or mastery of the course content. You may have had difficulty taking tests in the past, and because of these experiences, you may be convinced in advance that you'll do poorly. As you wait for the teacher to hand out the test, you begin to feel nervous and frightened, and with each passing minute your nervousness and fear intensify. By the time you finally look at the test, you're so upset that you "can't see straight." You may know the material "backward and forward," but your anxiety causes your mind to go blank. You may see questions you should be able to answer, but because the questions may be posed differently from what you had expected, you think that the test is covering material you never studied. You "clutch," and in your panic you forget everything you've learned. Your expectations of disaster quickly become a *self-fulfilling prophesy.*

Becoming apprehensive and going into a panic before taking a test can even cause you to fail a test or to get a C– instead of the B or B+ you deserve. If you studied conscientiously, it would be unfair if all of your hard work was undermined because of nervousness and anxiety.

If you continually panic when you take tests and get lower grades than you deserve, you have two basic options:

Option 1: Accept the situation, resign yourself to becoming panicked, and continue to perform below your true ability.

Option 2: Take charge of the situation and learn how to control your anxiety.

If you select Option 2, you can take practical and positive steps to reduce your test anxiety. You'll note that Elena, the student in the case study, used several of these techniques.

Test Relaxation Techniques

1. Close your eyes and slowly take several deep breaths while waiting for the test to be handed out. (Do not take more than three breaths because this could cause you to become dizzy.)

2. Keep your eyes closed and form a picture in your mind of you looking at the questions, knowing the answers, taking the test, doing well, and feeling proud and confident.

3. Silently recite and repeat positive statements about doing well while you're waiting for the test to be handed out. For example, you could remind yourself that you know the material, that you've studied conscientiously, that you're smart, and that you deserve to do well on the test.

4. With your eyes closed, let your body relax and let the fear and stress flow out. Imagine that your anxiety is located in a particular place in you body such as your chest, throat, or stomach. Focus your attention on this spot, and imagine your stress ebbing away.

5. To improve your confidence, select an easy question to answer first.

Anxiety and stage fright are quite common. Many talented professional actors, dancers, and musicians have bouts of nervousness before they begin to perform. Realizing that they must somehow conquer their fear, most figure out a system that helps them cope with their anxiety and go on with the show. In most cases, the butterflies go away as the performance progresses.

Professional athletes also are susceptible to anxiety before they go out onto the field, the court, the gymnastics arena, or the ice-skating rink. Most of these athletes develop procedure for calming themselves down so that they can function optimally. The same is true about test anxiety. Once you begin to answer the questions and discover that you know the answers, your anxiety will lessen.

The relaxation techniques described here should help you to get your anxiety under control and maximize your test performance. If you are prone to apprehension and nervousness, make it a habit to go through these steps when you take tests. As your grades improve as a result of your new study skills, you'll probably discover that your test anxiety will decrease.

TESTING YOUR MASTER STUDY PLAN

In the exercise on pages 100–101 of Unit 5, you did an experiment to see if you could improve your grades by eliminating distractions when studying. It would now be useful to do another, more comprehensive experiment. This experiment asks you to apply *all* the Study Max procedures you've learned up to this point. For the next two weeks, do a simple two-part experiment and see if it improves your work in school. *Remember:* for the experiment to be effective, you must make a commitment to follow through with using the procedures every day.

MASTER STUDY PLAN EXPERIMENT

Part 1: Make sure that you've studied smart. At the end of each day, check the smart thinking and studying steps you've used.

Effective Studying Checklist

	YES	NO
I realistically target the grade I want to receive on each assignment.	___	___
I realistically target the grade I want to receive on each test.	___	___
I realistically target the semester grade I want to receive in each subject.	___	___
I've recorded my homework on my assignment sheet, or I've used the teacher's homework handout effectively.	___	___

	YES	NO
I've studied in a quiet place and reduced distractions (friends, TV, telephone, loud music, etc.).	___	___
I've planned ahead.	___	___
I've budgeted adequate time to complete my studying.	___	___
I've followed my study schedule.	___	___
I've studied sitting at a desk or a table.	___	___
I made sure that I had the necessary books and supplies.	___	___
I've organized my materials.	___	___
I've carefully checked over my work to make sure it's neat and legible.	___	___
I've carefully checked over my work to make sure I've eliminated as many mistakes as possible.	___	___
Whenever possible, I've capitalized on my learning strengths and natural abilities.	___	___
I've mind-mapped and/or taken textbook notes.	___	___
I've identified important information, and I've indicated details and concepts.	___	___
I've anticipated the questions my teacher is likely to ask on the next test.	___	___
I've made up practice tests.	___	___
I've handed in my completed assignments when they were due.	___	___
I'm keeping track of my performance and my grades.	___	___
I'm prepared to make adjustments in my study strategy if my grades fail to meet my expectations.	___	___
I've considered the potential consequences of my actions and decisions.	___	___

Part 2: Keeping track of your performance. You've done grade-tracking experiments in previous units. Now that you've completed the program, you might want to continue to keep track of your performance by recording on the following form your grades on tests, homework assignments, and in-class assignments.

Daily Grades

Date: _____

Subject	Tests	Report/Essays	Homework	In-class Work
_____	_____	_____	_____	_____
_____	_____	_____	_____	_____
_____	_____	_____	_____	_____
_____	_____	_____	_____	_____
_____	_____	_____	_____	_____

Do this experiment for two weeks. (Your teacher will distribute a form on which you can record your performance for ten days.) This will allow you to quickly determine whether your grades are improving. If you're pleased with the results, you can continue the experiment for as long as you want!

SOME FINAL WORDS

School success hinges on having the necessary skills to learn and study productively. It also hinges on your attitude and frame of mind. To be successful in school, you must want to be successful.

You've learned, practiced, and applied many powerful study skills, and you now possess the necessary tools to handle the challenges and obligations that you'll encounter in high school and beyond. These tools will allow you to work up to your full academic potential and will provide you with a competitive advantage, assuming, of course, that you're willing to deliberately and consistently use the tools.

Your teacher may have covered every unit in the Study Max Program, or because of limited time, he or she may have selected specific units to use in class. If your teacher did chose to examine selected topics and if you believe that you might benefit from working on other units that weren't covered in class, you may want to ask the teacher for copies of these lessons to do on your own. By so doing, you will be taking a proactive role in improving your skills and enhancing your education.

Let's take a look at the range of study skills that are taught in the Study Max Program.

The Nuts and Bolts of Productive Study Skills

- Planning ahead
- Managing study time and creating a study schedule
- Recording assignments accurately
- Having the necessary materials for studying and doing homework
- Creating an organized study environment
- Concentrating and working efficiently and productively

- Mind-mapping
- Taking notes from textbooks
- Indicating important information in notes
- Differentiating main ideas and details
- Asking questions while studying
- Reviewing the types of questions the teacher has asked on previous tests
- Capitalizing on learning strengths
- Using effective memory techniques
- Making up practice tests
- Tracking performance

You may not fully appreciate how much you've actually learned and how many productive study skills you've acquired. One thing is certain: If you make a habit of thinking, acting, and studying smart, your school performance will improve.

Like ice cream, school success is habit forming. Once you taste it, you'll want more. Some habits are bad. This one, however, is good! Eat all you want. You have permission to pig out on academic achievement, good grades, and pride.

Recommended Readings

Armstrong, T. (2000). *In their own way: Discovering and encouraging your child's multiple intelligences* (revised and updated). New York: J. P. Tarcher/Putnam.

Beamon, G. W. (2000). *Teaching with adolescent learning in mind.* Arlington Heights, IL: SkyLight.

Campbell, L. (2003). *Mindful learning: 101 proven strategies for student and teacher success.* Thousand Oaks, CA: Corwin Press.

Gardner, H. (1983). *Frames of mind: The theory of multiple intelligences.* New York: Basic Books.

Glasgow, N. A., & Hicks, C. D. (2003). *What successful teachers do: 91 research-based classroom strategies for new and veteran teachers.* Thousand Oaks, CA: Corwin Press.

Greene, L. J. (1998). *Finding help when your child is struggling in school.* New York: St. Martin's Press.

Greene, L. J. (2002a). *Roadblocks to learning: Understanding the obstacles that can sabotage your child's academic success.* New York: Warner Books.

Greene, L. J. (2002b). *Winning the study game: Learning how to succeed in school.* Minnetonka, MN: Peytral.

Greene, L. J. (2004). *Study wise: A program for maximizing your learning potential.* Upper Saddle River, NJ: Pearson/Prentice Hall.

Greene, L. J. (In press). *The resistant learner.* New York: St. Martin's Press.

Levine, M. D. (2002). *A mind at a time.* New York: Simon & Schuster.

Wolfe, P. (2001). *Brain matters: Translating research into classroom practice.* Alexandria, VA: Association for Supervision and Curriculum Development.

Index

**CORWIN
PRESS**

The Corwin Press logo—a raven striding across an open book—represents the union of courage and learning. Corwin Press is committed to improving education for all learners by publishing books and other professional development resources for those serving the field of K–12 education. By providing practical, hands-on materials, Corwin Press continues to carry out the promise of its motto: **"Helping Educators Do Their Work Better."**